Journey of the Unhealed

*A Self-Help Memoir on Childhood Sexual Assault,
Trauma Awareness, and Healing Through
Spiritual Transformation*

J. Denise

Library of Congress Control Number: 2024916075

ISBN: 979-8-9908323-0-5

Dedication

To my loving daughter,

I'm saddened that you witnessed aspects of my brokenness, yet your presence inspired me to embark on this healing journey. I hope you notice my growth and that it's something you can be proud of. The love I hold for you is unparalleled. You highlighted the best in me; becoming your mother was my salvation. You arrived at a moment when I needed to experience unconditional love the most. I promise always to show up and protect you. I love you, baby girl!

To My high school sweetheart,

I appreciate your presence and support, given in the best way you could. Your love and kindness will always hold a special place in my heart. I appreciate your hard work and dedication to our family. I'm forever grateful, I love you!

Acknowledgments

As I sit down to pen these acknowledgments, I'm grateful for the numerous individuals who have supported me throughout my journey. It has been a transformative experience, it wouldn't have been possible without the unwavering support, wisdom, and encouragement of many of my family and friends.

First and foremost, I extend my deepest thanks to my parents. I extend my gratitude for the life you've given me. I've learned that love is not always about the perfect expression of affection, but sometimes about the quiet, persistent presence that endures through life's challenges. I love you both, endlessly.

To my sisters, I am grateful to you both for being compassionate listeners and a haven when life felt overwhelming. Thank you for your consistent presence and for showing up when I needed you the most. Your love and understanding have provided immense comfort and strength throughout my journey.

My nephew (Darren), thank you for your endless humor and support, reminding me of the importance of laughter even in the darkest times. Thank you for the love. I am so grateful to you and for the bond we share.

My brothers, though our paths may not cross as often as I would like, the roles you have played in my life and your presence, have contributed to my journey in ways that I value. I am deeply thankful for both of you.

A special word of gratitude goes to my dear friend "Saunders". When I needed comfort, you were there not just with words, but with the warmth of a hug when it mattered most. Thank you for every moment of support and kindness.

I am deeply grateful to my childhood friend and mentor, Gentry Simmons, for being the first to read my book and providing invaluable, insightful feedback.

To all my friends and family who have been a part of this journey, thank you from the bottom of my heart and being part of my story.

Finally, thank you, the reader, for embarking on this journey with me. Your willingness to engage with my story means more than words can express. Thank you for your time, empathy, and openness to understanding a life outside your own.

Table of Contents

Preface

As I sit to write these words, I am aware of the vulnerability that comes with unveiling parts of my life marked by shadows to the light of public scrutiny. This book is not just a recounting of events; it is an offering, a piece of my soul laid bare on these pages, in the hope that it might touch others who have walked similar paths and felt the same pains.

This journey through my life is one I never envisioned sharing so openly. Yet, here I am, driven by a purpose that has grown stronger with time the desire to shed light on the complex interplay of trauma, attachment, and the relentless quest for love and validation that so many of us endure in silence. It is a tale of survival, the myriad ways a spirit can break and mend; and the profound resilience that lives in the human heart.

From the earliest days of my childhood, through the turbulent waters of adolescence and into the complexities of adulthood, the specter of sexual assault cast long shadows over my relationships and self-image. Each chapter peels back the layers of those experiences, not to dwell in the darkness but to illuminate the paths I've walked through pain, misunderstanding, and often, misplaced guilt, towards a horizon of healing and self-discovery.

This is a story of confronting the wounds inflicted by those who harmed me directly but also by those who let me walk alone through action or inaction when I needed guidance the most. It is about the difficult process of untangling the threads of my past from the fabric of my present, learning to set boundaries, and finally, putting myself at the center of my life.

In sharing my journey, I am aware of the delicate balance between shedding light on painful truths and preserving the privacy and dignity of all involved. Some names and identifying details have been altered, not to attempt to mask the truth but to focus on the essence of the experiences.

To those who see echoes of their own stories in mine, know that you are not alone. Though our paths may differ, the quest for healing and understanding is a common thread that binds us. It is my hope that in my reflections, you find moments of solidarity, glimpses of hope, and perhaps the courage to face your journey with a renewed sense of strength and purpose.

And to all readers, I extend my heartfelt gratitude for your willingness to embark on this journey with me. It is a path marked by tears, triumphs, darkness, and light. May we walk the pathway together with open hearts and minds, moving towards a deeper understanding of the impact of trauma and the incredible capacity for resilience and healing that lies within each of us?

With gratitude and hope,

J. Denise

CHAPTER ONE

Foundations

Innocence Lost

"Losing your innocence is not just a moment but a transformation, where the purity of childhood is overshadowed by the harsh realities of the world, leaving a lasting mark on the soul".

J. DENISE

During my childhood, I was incredibly outgoing and full of life. An innate desire to assist others and a deep well of empathy filled my heart from a young age. My compassionate nature was evident in every interaction, whether it was helping others with their homework, babysitting for family, or assisting my teachers in the classroom. I distinctly recall receiving the citizenship award in elementary school numerous times for my helpfulness.

It wasn't until later in life that I encountered the term "child empath," a description that resonated deeply with me. Child empath refers to a young person who exhibits an increased sensitivity to the emotions and energy of those around them. These children are highly intuitive and often deeply attuned to the feelings and experiences of those around them. They may exhibit traits such as empathy, compassion, and a strong desire to help others. Child empaths feel emotions intensely, sometimes to the point of becoming overwhelmed by the emotions of others. Early on, I acquired an understanding of others' emotions, often sensing their feelings before they were expressed. While this gift could be overwhelming at times, it also served as a guiding light throughout my formative years.

As I matured, my empathy only deepened. Even in my youth, I was recognized as a source of support and comfort during times of need. Despite my tender age, adults often commented on my wisdom and maturity, qualities that seemed beyond my years. It wasn't until adulthood that I fully appreciated the depth of my gift-empathy was not merely a trait but a profound calling that shaped every interaction and relationship in my life.

However, embracing my empathic nature also brought its share of challenges. My innocence radiated through moments of play with my dog and dolls; and even through staging pretend church services on Sunday mornings. Clad in my red robe, mimicking the performance of the pastor in church, I reveled in the joy of imagination. Even in my youth, I understood the allure of a fantasy world, where I could escape with my imaginary friends.

Being the eldest child with a significant age gap between my siblings, imaginative play became my means of entertainment. Attending church was enjoyable, often accompanying my dad or other relatives; I was baptized at five. At that time, I harbored aspirations of becoming a preacher. I couldn't interpret the bible; I only knew what I was taught. It was merely me mimicking the act of the preachers in the pulpit. I learned about Jesus' teachings on love, compassion, and forgiveness, emphasizing that God loves everyone unconditionally. Of course, a child's learning is direct and pure; I took everything at face value because I trusted that the adults were speaking the truth and knew more than I did.

My innocence led me to believe whatever I was told, although some of what I was taught felt contradictory. I had countless questions but felt stifled by the notion that questioning God was forbidden. Though I was eager to learn more about Christ, fear overshadowed my curiosity. Teachings about sin and the consequences of disobedience led me to fear God's punishment.

The idea of an all-seeing God who punishes bad behavior created anxiety rather than a sense of moral guidance. I yearned to confide in God about my experiences, yet I hesitated. The uncertainty of why God allowed these things to happen to me weighed heavily on my young mind. I couldn't comprehend why God didn't reveal what was happening to me to my mother or why He didn't stop it. I believed that God was angry with me and that I was facing punishment.

One day, as we turned onto the street, a sinking feeling settled in the pit of my stomach. The sight of the structure ahead sent a shiver down my spine. To my seven-year-old self, it resembled a grand white castle, but it was just a two- story house. Despite my hopes, I couldn't shake the uneasy feeling creeping over me as we pulled into the yard and got out of the vehicle. I began walking alongside my mother: I tried to suppress the rising nervousness, although I couldn't pinpoint its source. My stomach churned with a mix of apprehension and dread. Yet, the presence of my mother offered a bit of reassurance, softening my fear. We began approaching the door; my heart pounded in my chest. A glance upward revealed someone peering out from the second-story window, sending a wave of panic coursing through me. Desperately, I reached for my mother's hand, but she continued walking, oblivious to my silent plea.

Once inside, the sound of footsteps thundered down the stairs, accompanied by the beckoning calls of unseen voices. "Come on, let's go upstairs and play," they urged, their voices laced with an unsettling eagerness. They were two young boys who lived in the home. I believe they were around 10 and 11 years old at the time. I just remembered walking up the stairs, concentrating on each step instead of worrying about what could happen once we got in the room. Sighing inwardly, I resigned myself to the inevitable. Once we entered the room, I could hear my mom saying her goodbyes and she would return to pick me up later. My mother's departure only heightened my anxiety.

Pressing against the windowpane, I watched as she retreated to our car, leaving me behind. Panic rising within me, I called out to her, but she couldn't hear me. Alone and vulnerable, I felt the recognizable feeling of hands tugging at my dress, accompanied by laughter. I had become accustomed to their inappropriate touching over time, but this time it was different. I felt a body against mine thrusting back and forth. It was a strange sensation. Too young to recognize the body part pressing against me, he was thrusting back and forth behind me. There was no penetration, but I was so scared because this wasn't familiar, and I didn't know what would happen next. Thankfully, the ordeal ended as abruptly as it began, interrupted by the distant call of my name from downstairs. With a sense of relief, I just continued to stare out of the window. I wanted to cry so badly, but I would never let them see me cry. Yet, at that moment, something fundamental shifted within me. The realization: my mother, my protector, had left me.

However, as I grew older, I found myself struggling with memories of the unsettling experiences, wondering if things could have been different if I had reacted differently. These memories left me disliking dresses, convinced that they somehow caused trouble. Despite this fear, I couldn't voice what was happening to me; I feared judgment or blame for my choice of clothing. As I matured, I decided to avoid dresses whenever possible, except for occasions like church where it felt obligatory. The burden of carrying this secret weighed heavily on me, but I became adept at hiding my true feelings, afraid of being perceived as "too fast" or "grown" if I spoke out. The exact age the touching began is unclear, but the earliest memory was around six years old. The image of the little girl standing in front of the window has consumed me mentally for many years. I would dream about this day consistently throughout my life. I convinced myself it was just another vision.

Also, when I was around six, I started having vivid dreams and visions that felt incredibly real. It dawned on me that some of these dreams would later come true. Despite being highly intuitive, I didn't fully grasp the significance of these experiences until I was older. As a child, it was overwhelming, and I did not understand what was happening. Fear consumed me as I struggled to make sense of it all, convinced that somehow, I was the one causing the incidents to happen; I didn't want to be blamed or punished. I had secrets I was hiding. At this point, I learned to mask everything I was dealing with and became this shy little girl who hoped no one would discover the truth.

As I entered my teenage years, the visions and dreams intensified, becoming more frightening and overwhelming. I struggled to find ways to deal with them. The thought of sharing these experiences terrified me; I worried people would accuse me of fabricating stories or become upset if I revealed what I foresaw about them. Despite the signs I received, I felt lost and unable to manage my feelings.

In search of an escape, I turned to alcohol, taking advantage of the times my parents were away. I was careful to consume just enough to dull the visions without drawing attention. Later, I experimented with marijuana but found it only amplified my visions and my sense of paranoia, leading me to use it less frequently. I longed to flee from these experiences. Even though I sensed God's presence in my life from an early age, I wasn't ready to embrace it anymore. Instead, I followed the path many teenagers do, seeking refuge in partying and hanging out with my friends all the while making poor choices and placing myself in risky situations.

I never anticipated that those situations would result in me being sexually assaulted and molested by several men I knew and trusted until I was approximately 22 years old. While I won't delve into specifics about each incident, it's important to note that I didn't perceive any of them as better or worse than the others. Each of these experiences was traumatic. I've consistently placed the blame on myself, finding it simpler to cope by acting as if none of it ever took place. My parents remained unaware of the trauma I endured until I decided to break my silence in the midst of writing this book.

Family Fractures

"Family fractures cast long shadows, influencing relationships in future generations. These early wounds shape how we love, trust, and connect, often guiding us toward healing or perpetuating cycles of pain".

J. DENISE

Reflecting on my childhood relationship with my mother, I looked for her to be my protector, even when my dad was around. She always seemed capable of fixing anything in my tender eyes. I believe every child views their mother as somewhat of a superhero, given that mothers possess innate nurturing qualities. In many cases, the mother serves as the primary caregiver, the one we seek solace from in times of distress and anguish.

Mother-daughter relationships are complex and multifaceted, often characterized by a deep emotional bond intertwined with challenges. While I understood her love for me, it felt distant and inaccessible; my mother lacked affection and emotional presence. I longed for the same bond with her that my siblings had, but I often found myself competing for her attention and struggling to be heard. I constantly felt overlooked and invalidated. She seemed to trust others' words over mine as if my words held little weight in her eyes.

I would describe my relationship with my father as somewhat more affectionate. Yet, I often felt that he relied on me to support him more than he did for me emotionally. I sensed that I played more of a nurturing role in our dynamic. I, too, felt unheard by my father. He often disregarded my perspective, asserting his own and using his authority as an adult and my father to silence me. Even though my father lived elsewhere, he remained an involved parent; he compensated for his physical absence by providing for me materially.

Because I struggled with seeking validation from both my parents, I frequently questioned whether I could trust them to protect and support me when I needed them most. These were the simple desires I harbored as a child. Feeling this way, I honestly didn't believe anyone would believe me about the abuse. It might seem unfair, but it's how I felt, especially considering past instances where I spoke up about things, even minor ones, and wasn't believed, with my mother and father taking someone else's word instead. Despite maintaining my silence, I held onto the belief that my parents should instinctively understand my needs and recognize my pain. I struggled as a child to comprehend how neither of them noticed.

Be mindful of the low-maintenance child. Parents can become so focused on the child who require more attention that they may unintentionally overlook the quieter child. These children often grow up without a strong relationship with their parents. I never felt prioritized growing up, which I believe is why I'm so accepting of being second or pushed to the background. When a sibling is involved in sports, they often become the family's focal point. This dynamic is also particularly common in "glass children" those who have siblings with chronic illnesses. The sick child naturally receives much of the parents' attention, leaving the other child feeling invisible. These children tend to hide their true selves, feeling inadequate and unable to measure up. They might act out or go above and beyond to get their parents' attention, but if this is not acknowledged, the void and longing only grow.

In my attempts to gain my parents' attention, I acted out, my behavior changed immensely, yet these cries for help went unnoticed, often resulting in scolding or punishment. My parents rarely resorted to physical discipline for misbehavior. While composing this book, I still hadn't revealed any specifics to my parents, and I might choose never to do so, but they are aware that the sexual assaults occurred. I don't want to feel judged, defend myself, or be interrogated. The intention behind writing this book isn't to criticize or attack my family's parenting, but rather, the manifestation of what I perceive as my Divine Purpose. I won't share details with my parents or anyone in my family. I choose to let people believe what they want. This book represents my perspective on how I was treated and the emotions I experienced. I am solely writing from my viewpoint. Despite my reserved nature, I felt compelled to share my story.

Growing up in the early 80s, my generation was taught to keep family matters private, adhering to the notion of "What happens in this house stays in this house." A phrase often used to emphasize the importance of keeping family matters private and not discussing them outside of the household. However, perpetuating this cultural norm does more harm than good, preventing children from seeking help when needed. Given the silence surrounding abuse within my family, concealing my own experiences was effortless. Nevertheless, as I began receiving signs from a higher power urging me to tell my story, I struggled with feelings of inadequacy and the fear of judgment. I initially resisted, attempting to convince myself that my story held no significance. I was adamant about keeping my secrets hidden. No one, absolutely no one, deserved access to this part of me. I suppressed it so deeply within my mind that I remained detached from reality for most of my life.

Yet, as the divine messages grew more persistent, I realized I had no choice except to embrace this calling. Testing the waters by subtly hinting at my experiences, I was met with minimal response from family but found solidarity with others who shared similar journeys. Through meditation and reflection, I recognized the importance of sharing my story for healing and raising awareness of these issues. I understand that my narrative could serve as a means for others to embark on their healing journeys and shed light on an important topic.

Within the Black community, children's voices often go unheard. Society's emphasis on maintaining familial secrecy meant many of us struggled in silence, our experiences and emotions relegated to the shadows. This lack of validation and acknowledgment deeply affected us, leaving scars that often went unnoticed. In my culture, there is a strong emphasis on keeping family secrets, accompanied by a sense of blind loyalty. Blind loyalty within the context of the Black community intends to be a deeply ingrained commitment to supporting and protecting family members or community members, often without question or consideration of potential consequences. This loyalty may stem from historical experiences of oppression and the need for solidarity within the community.

However, it can also contribute to perpetuating harmful behaviors or maintaining silence about issues such as abuse, dysfunction, or injustice within families or communities. Blind loyalty can lead individuals to overlook flaws, ignore wrongdoing, or engage in actions they would otherwise find unacceptable. It's time to break this cycle of silence and ensure that every child's voice is heard and respected, creating a world where openness, empathy, and understanding prevail.

Transmission of trauma from one generation to the next, often through familial and societal systems, is known as generational trauma. Generational trauma can significantly influence parenting practices and family dynamics. When parents have experienced trauma themselves, whether directly or indirectly through their family history, it can impact how they interact with their children and navigate the challenges of parenting.

Family fractures cast long shadows, influencing relationships in future generations. These early wounds shape how we love, trust, and connect, often guiding us toward healing or perpetuating cycles of pain. One common effect of generational trauma on parenting is the transmission of unhealed wounds and unresolved emotions. Parents who have experienced trauma may struggle with emotional regulation, communication, and forming secure attachments with their children. They may unintentionally pass on patterns of behavior learned from their own traumatic experiences, such as avoidance of emotional expression or difficulty in establishing healthy boundaries. Additionally, generational trauma can shape parenting beliefs and attitudes. Parents may be more inclined to adopt authoritarian or permissive parenting styles because of their upbringing, which can impact their children's sense of safety, autonomy, and self- esteem. Moreover, trauma can influence parents' perceptions of risk and danger, leading to overprotectiveness, which may limit children's opportunities for exploration and growth.

However, it's important to note that generational trauma is not deterministic, and parents can break the cycle of trauma through awareness, healing, and intentional parenting practices. Seeking support through therapy, education, and community resources can help parents recognize and address the impact of trauma on their parenting, fostering resilience, empathy, and healthy relationships within the family. By doing so, parents can create a nurturing and supportive environment that promotes healing and empowers their children to thrive despite the challenges they may face.

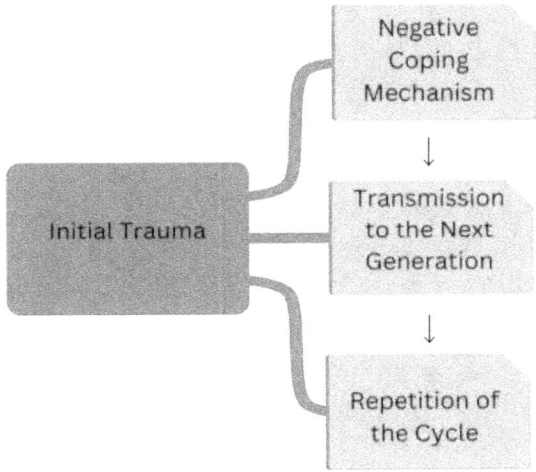

The cycle of generational trauma

In my family, the cycle of generational trauma revolves around different forms of abuse, resulting in fractured relationships between parents and their children. Someone must intervene to break this destructive pattern. The time has come to cease sweeping our issues under the rug and confront these generational curses head-on. Mothers and daughters are in constant conflict, intensified by the absence of a male presence in parenting and the scarcity of two-parent households. The lack of emotional connection and understanding compounds these challenges. Financial instability further exacerbates our struggles. While I anticipate resistance from my family regarding my decision to write this book and speak on issues within the family, we cannot begin to heal these deep wounds without first acknowledging them. I am fully committed to addressing these traumas within our lineage to facilitate healing and transformation.

I was raised in a household where my mother and stepfather were present. My stepfather consistently treated me as if I were his child. However, I still experienced a sense of emptiness from the absence of my biological father's daily presence. My father was always in relationships with women who had children, and I perceived that they received more of his attention due to my infrequent visits. He was a constant presence in their lives, often acting as a father figure to them, as many of them had absent fathers. When I was around, I had to share his attention, it left me feeling confused and longing. My stepfather was supportive, but it couldn't replace the need for my biological father.

If you grew up with parents living apart or one parent was absent, and frequently moved due to military assignments, evictions, instability, foster care, or any other reasons, identifying what *home* means can be challenging. Often, the mother becomes the primary caregiver, as was true for me. Sometimes, parents may not fully consider the impact of these varied living situations on their children. Kids need consistency - a consistent living situation, a sense of security, a life free from constant turmoil, structured routines, and nurturing care. While parents may provide ample love and material comforts, a lack of underlying stability can still lead to a sense of longing.

The relationship between my mother and I is a significant challenge that requires repair. I believe I began to lose connection with my mother early on due to my inability to trust that she could provide protection. Not to absolve my father of responsibility; however, mothers have a unique nurturing quality that was absent during my upbringing. I trust my mother did her best to protect me given the circumstances. However, I never confided in her about my trauma.

The day she left me behind, a part of me lost faith in her, and I struggled to trust her again. This strained our bond, worsened by her unresolved trauma, resulting in her emotional unavailability. The lack of feeling protected by one's parents can have profound and lasting effects on a child's relationship, shaping their perceptions, emotions, and behaviors. Here's how this lack of protection can impact a child's relationship with their parents:

Trust and Attachment: When a child does not feel protected by their parents, their trust in them can be eroded. Trust is the foundation of any relationship, and when a child perceives their parents as unable or unwilling to provide safety and security, it can lead to a breakdown in trust. This may result in a reluctance to confide in or rely on their parents for support, leading to a weakened bond between child and parent.

Emotional Distance: The absence of a sense of protection can create emotional distance between a child and their parents. They feel abandoned or neglected by those who are supposed to care for them, which can lead to resentment, anger, or withdrawal. A child may distance themselves emotionally from their parents as a way of self- preservation, fearing further disappointment or rejection.

Low Self-Esteem and Insecurity: A lack of parental protection can contribute to low self-esteem and insecurity in a child. When a child's basic need for safety is not met, they may internalize feelings of worthlessness or inadequacy, believing that they are unworthy of love or care. This can manifest in various ways, such as seeking validation from external sources or engaging in self-destructive behaviors.

Difficulty Forming Healthy Relationships: Children who do not feel protected by their parents may struggle to form healthy relationships with others later in life. The early experiences of feeling abandoned or betrayed by those closest to them can shape their expectations of relationships, leading to patterns of distrust, fear of intimacy, or difficulty in establishing boundaries.

Resentment and Estrangement: In some cases, the lack of protection from parents can lead to feelings of resentment or estrangement. A child may harbor deep-seated anger towards their parents for failing to fulfill their role as protectors, leading to a strained or distant relationship. In extreme cases, the child may choose to sever ties with their parents altogether to protect themselves from further emotional harm.

Overall, the impact of not feeling protected by my parents influenced my sense of self, the ability to trust others, and the capacity to form healthy, fulfilling relationships throughout my life. After becoming a mother to my daughter, I became aware of the generational trauma within me. I found myself being excessively protective but lacking in displays of affection toward her; I could provide for her material needs, but there was a noticeable absence of emotional stability in our relationship. Despite my intentions to be more engaged as a parent, I failed to recognize how deeply my trauma had impacted me. It wasn't until I noticed resistance from my daughter that I realized I was projecting my pain onto her.

There was an encounter once, my daughter wanted to cuddle with me, but I found myself pushing her away. Affection does not come naturally to me. Despite her persistent efforts, the tug-of-war between us triggered deep-seated emotions, causing me to disconnect from the present moment. It felt as though she was another person trying to invade my space, triggering memories of past attacks and leaving me feeling defenseless. I couldn't shake the sense of helplessness in my efforts to establish boundaries. This was my daughter, yet I couldn't escape the overload of emotions. My inner child emerged; I felt the desire to call out to my mother, to make it all stop. The embarrassment was real as I grappled with the realization that my child couldn't comprehend the turmoil within me, only sensing my rejection.

Determined to break the cycle, I committed to address and heal from my trauma. My healing journey will enable me to support other family members and contribute to healing on a broader scale, within my community and beyond. The presence of a stable family structure can significantly impact a child's sense of safety and security. Recognizing that my parents have experienced significant hardships and trauma in their own lives was the first step. Forgiving my parents for projecting their trauma onto me involved a deep and challenging process of understanding and empathy. It required acknowledgment that my parents, like all others, are products of their own experiences, including any trauma they may have endured and never disclosed. Understanding that they were doing the best they could with the resources and coping strategies they had at the time softened my feelings of resentment or anger. However, knowing that holding onto resentment or blame may only perpetuate the cycle of pain and dysfunction.

Reflecting on how my parents' trauma has influenced my thoughts, feelings, and behaviors is pivotal; it allows me to identify patterns that I may wish to change and take proactive steps toward personal growth and healing. Breaking the cycle of generational trauma often requires support from others, whether through therapy, support groups, or trusted friends and mentors. Forgiveness doesn't mean I am excusing or minimizing the impact of my parents' actions. Instead, it's a conscious decision to release myself from the burden of carrying resentment and reclaim my power to create a different future for myself and future generations. Establishing boundaries that prioritize my well-being and protect myself and my kid from further harm is essential. Breaking the cycle of generational trauma, particularly in the context of childhood sexual assault, involves a multi-faceted approach that includes awareness, education, and proactive measures to prevent abuse.

CHAPTER TWO

Signs and Prevention

Recognizing the Signs

The term sexual assault or sexual abuse refers to any form of sexual contact that occurs without the direct consent of the victim. This can encompass a wide range of behaviors, including unwanted touching, groping, fondling, rape, or other forms of sexual coercion or violence. A person who commits sexual assault may be referred to as a rapist, molester, or perpetrator. It's important to emphasize that sexual assault is a serious crime that violates a person's rights and autonomy, and perpetrators can face legal consequences for their actions. The terms molestation and rape are often used to describe similar incidents, yet they refer to distinct forms of sexual assault. Molestation generally involves inappropriate touching or fondling of a sexual nature without consent. Rape, on the other hand, specifically refers to the act of forced sexual intercourse against someone's will. These violations can occur at any age.

It's key for adults to recognize and understand that children's sexual curiosity is a normal part of their development, particularly during puberty when their bodies undergo significant changes. However, distinguishing between natural sexual curiosity and potentially abusive behaviors can be challenging. Natural sexual curiosity often involves age-appropriate exploration of one's body, asking questions about sexuality, and seeking information about sexual topics. It is typically not secretive or coercive and occurs within appropriate boundaries. On the other hand, potentially abusive behaviors may involve secrecy, manipulation, coercion, or exploitation. For instance, a child might display indications of distress, fear, or discomfort when being coerced into sexual activities with another individual. They might also exhibit inappropriate awareness or curiosity about sexual matters beyond their developmental stage or demonstrate behaviors that imitate adult sexual conduct.

In my experience with the two young boys, this wasn't a mutual situation where kids were curious about what the opposite sex may have, you know, "Let me see yours, and I'll let you see mine." I never enjoyed what was happening, nor did I understand why it was happening. I just knew there was a possibility it was going to happen. Some may question whether the boy's comprehension was extensive enough to understand what they were doing was wrong. Rightfully, given the age gap and developmental differences, this is strongly indicative of sexual assault. A child molester can be anyone. including individuals within a child's peer group or even siblings. Parents and caregivers must be vigilant and aware of potential risks, regardless of the perpetrator's relationship with the child. This underscores the importance of educating children about body safety, boundaries, and consent and fostering open communication, so they feel comfortable reporting inappropriate behavior, regardless of who the perpetrator may be.

Parents do their best to protect their children, but sometimes they may not completely succeed. This isn't always a result of negligence; because parents leave their children with people they truly trust. It's challenging for a parent to contemplate the possibility of their child becoming a target or being subjected to any form of abuse, especially considering the precautions taken to ensure their safety. The statistics on child sexual abuse are concerning, with many cases perpetrated by trusted family members. According to the CDC, approximately one in four girls and one in 13 boys experience some form of sexual abuse in the United States. However, it's important to recognize that these figures represent only reported cases. Children between the ages of seven and 13 are particularly vulnerable to sexual abuse, and perpetrators often exploit their trust and familiarity with the child. It's important to understand that sexual abuse occurs due to decisions made by the abuser rather than any trait in the child.

It's essential to emphasize that children should never be blamed for any abuse they experience. Nevertheless, specific factors can elevate a child's vulnerability to being targeted for sexual abuse. These include unmonitored access to technology, disabilities, non- verbal communication, low self-esteem, exposure to domestic violence in the home, and living in blended families, among others. To protect children from sexual abuse, caregivers and communities need to be vigilant and proactive in creating safe environments for children to thrive.

This includes educating children about body safety and boundaries, fostering open communication, monitoring their online activities, and providing support and resources for children who may be at risk or have experienced abuse. Child predators share a common goal: to exploit and victimize children for their sexual gratification. They often present themselves as friendly and charming individuals, and they come from diverse backgrounds, including various ethnicities, races, and socioeconomic statuses. Predators frequently seek out environments where they can have close contact with children, such as churches, schools, parks, and sports activities.

Single mothers and their children may be particularly vulnerable to predators, as perpetrators often target households where there is a lack of male presence or support. Some Single mothers face financial challenges, and predators may exploit this vulnerability by offering financial assistance or resources in exchange for access to the mother or her children. Predators may exploit single mothers' emotional needs, offering companionship, affection, or validation to gain their trust and manipulate them or their children. Single mothers may be overwhelmed or distracted, making it easier for predators to gain access to their children. Overall, predators exploit single mothers due to a combination of perceived vulnerabilities, limited support networks, financial strain, emotional needs, and social isolation. It's important for single mothers to be aware of these risks and to seek support from trusted individuals. Research suggests that children raised in single-parent households may face a higher risk of exposure to sexual abuse compared to those in two-parent homes.

When a predator begins to assault a child sexually, their behavior and character towards the child can change in several disturbing ways, often centered around manipulating and controlling the child. Here are some common changes:

Grooming: The perpetrator might initially act very kindly towards the child, giving them gifts or special attention to gain their trust and create a sense of debt or loyalty.

Secrecy: The abuser may start to encourage secrecy, framing their interactions as special secrets that should not be shared with others. This can be a method to isolate the child and make it harder for them to seek help.

Threats and Coercion: As the abuse continues, the abuser might use threats or coercion to keep the child silent. This could involve threats to harm the child and their loved ones or even threats of punishment if the child tells anyone about the abuse.

Blaming the Child: The perpetrator might manipulate the child into believing that they are responsible for the abuse or that they initiated it, which can cause confusion and guilt in the child.

Behavioral Shifts: The abuser might become more controlling, monitoring the child's activities closely and limiting their interactions with others to maintain control over the situation.

Emotional Manipulation: There might be an alternation between kindness and cruelty; the abuser may be affectionate at times and extremely harsh at others, which can be emotionally destabilizing for the child.

Creating Opportunities to Be Alone: The abuser may manipulate situations to ensure they are alone with the child more frequently. This can include offering to babysit, taking the child on trips alone, or creating situations where the child is left alone with them at home.

Monitoring and Controlling Behaviors: The abuser might start to control more aspects of the child's life, from what they wear and eat to who they can talk to and what they are allowed to do, further reducing the child's autonomy and ability to seek help.

Isolation: Isolating the child is a common tactic used by abusers. This might involve making excuses to keep the child away from friends, family, or social activities where others might notice signs of distress or where the child might disclose the abuse. The abuser might portray themselves as the only true protector or friend the child has, thereby increasing the child's dependency on them.

These signs and behavioral changes can also apply to siblings or peers who sexually abuse their siblings. It's important to be vigilant for any shift in behavior or dynamics among children, as these can be indicators of abuse within familial or peer relationships. These behaviors are manipulative strategies designed to create an environment where the child feels completely under the control and influence of the abuser, reducing the likelihood of the abuse being discovered and increasing the child's sense of helplessness. It's important to recognize these signs as potential red flags for abuse. It's important to recognize that predators can be of any gender, although many convicted predators are men. Some female predators facilitate access for their partners to victimize children. This dynamic is often observed in situations where a female caregiver, such as a mother or guardian, knowingly allows or even encourages her partner to engage in abusive behavior with children in the household.

In some instances, female and male predators may have been victims of abuse themselves, leading to complex psychological dynamics where they may enable or participate in abusive behaviors. Female predators may fear repercussions or rely on their partners for financial or emotional support, making it difficult for them to intervene or seek help. Predators often employ manipulative tactics, such as grooming, to gain the trust of both the child and their family. Grooming involves behaviors like giving gifts, providing special attention, isolating the child from others, and gradually crossing physical boundaries.

Scenario: Grooming

In this scenario, I explore the subtle and insidious process of grooming by a stepfather. Mark, recently married to Samantha, has become the stepfather to 10-year-old Amanda. Amanda, an introverted child wrestling with the emotional aftermath of her parents' divorce, finds herself increasingly drawn to Mark's attentive and understanding demeanor. Samantha, preoccupied with balancing her new marriage and work, trusts Mark to be a supportive presence; Mark starts to gradually manipulate Amanda. What begins as seemingly innocent acts of kindness and attention slowly escalate into a series of calculated behaviors designed to isolate, confuse, and exploit Amanda. This scenario aims to shed light on the steps of grooming, emphasizing the importance of awareness and intervention to protect vulnerable children.

Background:

- **Stepparent:** Mark, the stepfather to Amanda, a 10-year-old girl.

- **Child:** Amanda, who is naturally introverted and has recently been struggling with her parents' divorce.

- **Setting:** Mark and Samantha, Amanda's mother has been married for six months, and Mark has moved into their family home.

Stages of Grooming:
Step 1: Targeting the Child

- **Behavior:** Mark notices that Amanda often plays alone and seems withdrawn from her peers and family members.

- **Action:** He takes an interest in her hobbies and offers to spend time doing activities she enjoys, like drawing and playing video games.

Step 2: Gaining Trust and Information

- **Behavior:** Mark frequently engages Amanda in conversations, asking her about her feelings, friends, and even her insecurities.

- **Action:** He uses this information to portray himself as a trustworthy adult who understands and sympathizes with her more than others.

Step 3: Isolation

- **Behavior:** Mark begins suggesting that Amanda spends more time at home rather than going out with friends or participating in extracurricular activities.

- **Action:** He might say things like, "You're safer here with me," or "I enjoy our time together more than they do."

Step 4: Creating Secrecy

- **Behavior:** Mark starts small secrets with Amanda, like letting her stay up late to watch movies, telling her, "Don't tell your mom, she might not understand our fun."

- **Action:** This establishes a 'special' bond that excludes other family members, particularly the custodial parent.

Step 5: Desensitization to Touch

- **Behavior:** Physical contact begins with 'innocent' touches, like brushing her hair or a hand on the back.

- **Action:** Gradually, these touches become more frequent and intimate, normalizing his physical presence.

Step 6: Introduction of Sexual Content

- **Behavior:** Mark might introduce sexual content subtly, perhaps through movies or jokes that are inappropriate for Amanda's age.

- **Action:** This serves to test Amanda's reaction and further normalize discussions and imagery that are sexual in nature.

Step 7: Full Exploitation

- **Behavior:** Once Amanda is isolated, emotionally dependent, and desensitized to touch and sexual content, Mark moved to outright abuse.

- **Action:** He relies on the established secrecy and Amanda's confusion and fear to keep her silent.

Conclusion:

This scenario outlines a potential grooming process by a stepfather, which is often gradual and escalates in severity. The intent is to manipulate the child into compliance and secrecy. Recognizing early signs of grooming can help prevent escalation to abuse.

One concerning aspect is when teachers, who hold positions of trust and authority, exploit their access to children for grooming purposes. Teachers may use their influence, rapport with students, and access to school facilities to manipulate and groom children for abuse. For example, a teacher may offer special attention, praise, or alter grades for a student to create a sense of dependence and loyalty. They may gradually escalate the level of physical contact or emotional intimacy under the guise of mentorship or friendship. Parents, educators, and communities must remain vigilant and aware of the signs of grooming behavior. This includes maintaining open communication with children about appropriate boundaries, teaching them about personal safety, and encouraging them to speak up if they feel uncomfortable or threatened by someone's actions. Additionally, institutions such as schools should consider implementing comprehensive policies and training programs to prevent, identify, and respond to instances of grooming and abuse by educators.

Recognizing Grooming Behaviors: Grooming involves the abuser slowly winning over the trust of the victim and their family or establishing an emotional bond to gain increased access to the child. Understanding these tactics can help in identifying potentially dangerous situations early. Here are some common grooming tactics:

- **Special Attention and Treatment:** The abuser may single out a child for special attention, praise, gifts, or treats, making the child feel special and valued.

- **Isolation:** The abuser may try to isolate the child from their peers or family members, creating a situation where the child becomes dependent on the abuser for social interaction and support.

- **Filling a Need:** They often look for vulnerabilities such as loneliness, low self-esteem, or family problems and position themselves as the only person who understands and supports the child.

- **Secrecy:** The abuser might encourage the child to keep secrets from their parents or guardians, framing it as a special bond between them. This secrecy can be about small things at first, to test and build the child's willingness to hide information.

- **Desensitization to Touch:** Gradual introduction of physical contact, starting with seemingly innocent touch and slowly moving to more invasive forms of contact. This desensitizes the child to being touched and blurs the boundaries of appropriate physical interaction.

- **Material Gifts:** Giving gifts or providing privileges that the child's parents or guardians might not offer. This can include toys, money, or access to activities and experiences the child values.

- **Role of Protector or Mentor:** Taking on a role of mentorship, guidance, or protection, making the child feel cared for and safe, and often filling a gap perceived in the child's life.

- **Threats and Manipulation:** As the grooming progresses, the abuser might use threats or manipulation to keep the child compliant, often suggesting that the child will be blamed, not believed, or that disclosure will result in negative consequences for the child or their loved ones.

- **Technology and Online Grooming:** Utilizing social media, chat rooms, and other online platforms to befriend and manipulate children in an environment where guardians are less likely to monitor interactions. This can include sending messages, sharing images or videos, and encouraging the child to engage in similar behavior.

Signs of sexual assault or abuse can manifest both physically and emotionally. Below, I've outlined some warning signs, drawing from my personal experiences, knowledge, and research. It's important to remember that not every sign may apply to your child. There are numerous indicators of abuse, so parents and guardians must educate themselves about these signs to determine if their child might be displaying any symptoms of abuse. However, it's also important to note that these signs alone do not definitively indicate abuse but should prompt further observation and attention.

Physical Signs

- Unexplained injuries or bruises, especially around the genital or anal areas.
- Difficulty walking or sitting, which may indicate physical trauma.
- Changes in hygiene, such as refusing to bathe or bathing excessively.
- Signs of sexually transmitted infections (STIs) or symptoms related to genital infections.
- Pregnancy, especially in adolescents who might not be expected to be sexually active.

Behavioral and Emotional Signs

- Changes in behavior or personality, such as becoming withdrawn, aggressive, or clingy.
- Their outward appearance might alter. They may avoid wearing certain clothing items they once enjoyed.
- You might observe a reluctance to wear clothes that expose their body, with boys or girls opting for more layers or loose-fitting garments.
- Regression to earlier developmental stages, including bed-wetting or thumb-sucking.

- Changes in eating habits, which could include sudden weight gain or loss or signs of an eating disorder.

- Sleep disturbances, such as nightmares, difficulty falling asleep, or fear of being alone at night.

- Sudden decline in academic performance or loss of interest in school and extracurricular activities.

- Excessive knowledge of sexual topics inappropriate for the child's age or new words for body parts.

- Fear of certain places, people, or activities, particularly being alone with a specific individual.

- Unexplained gifts or money which might indicate grooming behavior by an abuser.

- Self-harm or talk of suicide, especially in older children and teenagers.

- Observe how your child interacts with action figures or dolls. You might detect unusual behavior, such as mimicking actions they have experienced or displaying aggressive or abusive behavior towards them.

- The child begins sexually exploiting other kids. They may mimic the behavior of the abuser on their younger siblings or peers.

Psychological Signs

- Anxiety and depression, which may manifest as sadness, withdrawal from friends and family, or loss of interest in activities they once enjoyed.

- Post-traumatic stress disorder (PTSD) symptoms, such as flashbacks, being easily startled, or having frequent nightmares.

- Low self-esteem, which may be evident in how the child speaks about themselves or their body.

- Avoidance of touch or physical affection, or conversely, inappropriate sexual behavior or language that is not age appropriate.

Teacher-Student Grooming: A Case Study of Nikki

Background: Nikki, a 12-year-old middle school student, lived in a suburban neighborhood with her mother and younger brother. A bright and curious child, Nikki participated in various school clubs and enjoyed her after-school art class the most.

Introduction to the Groomer: Nikki met Mr. Williams, a volunteer assistant in her art class in his late twenties. Mr. Williams was well-liked by students for his friendly approach and was known for giving extra attention to those who showed interest and talent in art.

Grooming Process:

1. **Targeting the Victim:** Mr. Williams noticed Nikki's dedication and often praised her work extravagantly in front of the class, making her feel special.

2. **Gaining Trust and Information:** Over several weeks, he asked Nikki about her family, her interests outside of school, and her aspirations. Learning about her father's recent departure and her mother's busy work schedule, Mr. Williams positioned himself as a supportive adult figure.

3. **Filling a Need:** Recognizing the lack of a father figure in her life, Mr. Williams offered Nikki additional help after classes, further cementing his role as a trusted

adult. He listened to her problems, offered advice, and even bought her small gifts related to her artistic interests.

4. **Isolating the Child:** Mr. Williams suggested that Nikki could benefit from private lessons at his home studio to prepare for a local youth art competition, which seemed like a great opportunity for Nikki. He also discouraged her from discussing these lessons with others, framing it as a "special secret" that would be a wonderful surprise once her improved skills were revealed at the competition.

5. **Secrecy and Desensitization to Touch:** During their private sessions, Mr. Williams began to share more personal stories with Nikki, building a deeper emotional connection. He occasionally touched her in ways that seemed innocent but gradually became more inappropriate, like adjusting her posture by holding her shoulders or touching her hair.

Discovery and Intervention: Nikki's mother noticed a change in her behavior; Nikki became more secretive, and her mood fluctuated more than usual. After seeing messages from Mr. Williams on Nikki's phone that were overly affectionate, her mother questioned Nikki, who initially resisted but eventually disclosed everything. Horrified, her mother contacted the school and law enforcement.

Outcome: An investigation was initiated, revealing that Mr. Williams had been flagged at another school for similar behavior but had not been formally charged. Nikki stopped attending the art class, and Mr. Williams was barred from volunteering in the school district. Nikki began therapy to help her process her experiences.

Lessons Learned: This case study highlights the importance of recognizing grooming behaviors that start as seemingly benign interactions but slowly cross boundaries into inappropriate territory. It underscores the need for parents and educators to maintain open lines of communication with children about their day-to-day experiences and to be vigilant about adults who take an excessive interest in a child.

If you notice any of these signs in a child, it's important to approach the situation with sensitivity and care. Encourage open communication without leading questions and consider seeking help from professionals who specialize in dealing with child abuse and trauma.

Steps Towards Prevention

Parents need to be vigilant and proactive in understanding and safeguarding their children from potential predators. By staying informed about the risks and warning signs associated with child predators, parents can take preventive measures to protect their children's safety and well-being. This includes educating children about boundaries, online safety, and recognizing and reporting inappropriate behavior.

Additionally, fostering open communication and trust within the family can encourage children to confide in their parents about any concerns or encounters they may have with individuals who pose a threat. Ultimately, parental involvement and awareness play a necessary role in creating a safe environment where children can thrive and remain protected from harm. Teaching children to be wary of strangers and recognizing common predator's lures is helpful.

According to Child Lures Prevention, predators use various tactics to lure children, including affection, pets, assistance, authority, bribery, ego/fame, fun and games, emergencies, heroism, job opportunities, name recognition, playmates/companions, pornography, threats and weapons, on-line interactions, drugs, and hate and violence. Parents should educate their children about these lures and empower them to assert boundaries and seek help if they feel uncomfortable or threatened. Moreover, fostering open communication and maintaining vigilance can help prevent children from becoming victims of sexual abuse.

These are the 17 most common lures predators use:

The Affection Lure

This happens at the hands of someone the child knows when the child has been neglected by a caretaker and starved of affection.

The Pet Lure

Most kids love animals. They will use the "lost puppy" trick or show the kids a new or exotic animal.

The Assistant Lure

Predators may seek help from the kid. This could be help carrying a package or pretending to be disabled to seek assistance walking to the car.

The Authority Lure

Predators who are in authoritarian positions will use their positions to take advantage of the kids by use of intimidation.

The Bribery Lure

This one is well-known and still works. They will offer candy, gifts, toys, money, etc.

The Ego/Fame Lure

They will promise some form of spotlight for the child to gain awareness in their chosen artistry such as modeling contracts, scholarships, rap/singing contracts, etc. They may create bogus auditions or photo shoots in a secret location.

The Fun and Games Lure

They will play games that will give them close access to the kids, such as tickling and wrestling. This also includes games where they use restraints such as handcuffs and ropes.

The Emergency Lure

Predators use this to manipulate children by fabricating an urgent situation or crisis. Predators may fake illness, injury, or other emergencies to coerce children into complying with their demands. This lure preys on children's instinct to help others.

The Hero Lure

The predator can be someone who the child views as a hero. This could be a teacher, coach, or local celebrity. The child will be very comfortable with this individual.

The Job Lure

The offering of high-paying job. They may create a fake position and interview. They can run an ad seeking a pet-sitting or babysitting position.

The Name Recognition Lure

Placing name tags on backpacks, lunch boxes, or any other belongings of the child allows predators to call the child by name.

The Playmate/Companion Lure

Predators will involve their kids or other kids to lure in potential victims. Sleepovers, play dates, and parties are breeding grounds for potential assault. Most often, they will create an environment of no boundaries, and anything goes, which can be alluring to children.

The Pornography Lure

Pornography is used since kids are curious about sex. It wouldn't be too difficult to hold their attention with videos, magazines, and pictures.

The Threats and Weapons Lure

Sometimes predators may use weapons or violence to lure kids and then intimidate them to keep them from talking by saying, "No one will believe you."

The Computer/On-line Lure

Predators use online chat and social media platforms. They create accounts as minors in hopes of befriending kids to get their personal information to possibly meet them.

The Drug Lure

Predators will use drugs and alcohol to lure kids into abuse.

The Lure of Hate and Violence.

Predators also target kids with anger issues whose rage feeds off prejudice against other races, cultures, and sexual orientations.

In summary, preventing child sexual abuse requires a comprehensive approach that includes educating children about appropriate and inappropriate behavior, establishing open lines of communication so they feel safe reporting anything unusual, and maintaining vigilance to notice signs of abuse. Additionally, adults should be trained to recognize potential lures and grooming behaviors by perpetrators, ensuring they can intervene before abuse occurs. This multi-layered strategy helps to create a protective environment around children, reducing their risk of abuse.

Create A Safe Space: As parents, we must ensure our children feel they can openly talk to us; it is important to establish a space where they feel safe to share their thoughts and concerns. With the hustle and bustle of life, such as juggling multiple children, work, and activities, it can be challenging to find time, it's imperative to be present and attentive to the subtle changes in our children's behaviors and actions.

Growing up, I experienced a lack of being heard, which led me to feel isolated and unwilling to share, especially about the abuse—raising children in the same manner as our parents may not be as effective with the current generation, which faces different challenges and exposures. Effective communication is key for prevention. With access to social media and the Internet, children today are exposed to various influences. Online pornography and realistic sexual content in gaming systems further complicate matters. Predators take advantage of these platforms, posing as peers to exploit children. Awareness equips them to navigate safely and feel empowered to disclose any concerns.

Educating our children and encouraging open dialogue can significantly enhance their safety and willingness to speak up about uncomfortable situations. Creating this open line of communication early is pertinent, as children's desire for privacy grows with age. Casual conversations during car rides, mealtimes, or relaxed weekend chats can open up opportunities for dialogue. Using open-ended questions rather than yes/no inquiries can elicit more detailed responses, helping to gauge if your child has been in uncomfortable situations or how they might handle them.

Consider asking your child hypothetical questions if you're concerned, they may have been sexually violated, or to understand how they might react in such situations: "What would you do if a friend told you a secret that made them uncomfortable, something they felt they couldn't share with their parents or anyone else? How would you respond? Is there anyone you feel safe sharing your secrets with?" Engaging in conversations like these with your children is important. Ensure your questions are appropriate for their age and comprehension level. Listening to and connecting with your child is useful. For many parents, including myself, resisting the urge to react, offer opinions, or pass judgment immediately can be challenging, but it's needed for building trust. Your response matters greatly, especially in delicate situations; encourage your child to ask questions, ensuring the discussion matches their understanding.

It's also important to be mindful of the messages we convey about protection and consequences. Statements like "I'd go to jail about you," "I'll kill anyone that messes with you," "I'll die for you," or any other similar phrases used by parents to reassure their child of unwavering protection. Consider, however, the impact of such a declaration. Would your child feel at ease confiding in you about being harmed if they believed it could result in losing you? This might deter a child from sharing their experiences out of fear of you not being around. Most children have a protective instinct towards their parents and might withhold information to avoid causing trouble. Likewise, if the individual in question is someone the child holds dear and respects, they wouldn't wish harm upon them either.

It's a great idea to note that 91% of abuse occurs at the hands of someone the child knows well or has interacted with. I consistently remind my daughter that if anyone, including myself, makes her feel uncomfortable, she has the right to speak up and not hesitate to inform me. I highlight without her sharing, I'm unable to offer protection. My role is to be her mother, her protector, and I sincerely hope she perceives me as such. I assure her that even if someone threatens to harm me or suggests that her words won't be believed, she should still confide in me. I make it a point to continually affirm that I will always believe her and ensure that no harm will come our way; emphasizing that she can talk to me about anything, even if it involves someone she knows and loves, is essential. Assuring your child of your belief and support regardless of the situation is crucial for maintaining an open and trusting relationship. Despite our best efforts, some children may still find it hard to open up about abuse due to fear of judgment, embarrassment, or disbelief.

However, a foundation of trust and open communication can make a significant difference. I hope that every child has someone they trust enough to confide in. If your child isn't ready to talk, don't pressure them into a conversation. They'll speak when they're ready. My deepest hope is that at least one parent will be the confidante for their child. I understand the importance of this deeply, as I once had no one to turn to. I was that child, the one who kept silent no matter what. However, the knowledge I've shared in this book provides the foundation I longed for in my experiences. Perhaps with that, I might have found the courage to speak up.

Set Boundaries. If your child is naturally playful, friendly, and shows a lot of affection, it's important to teach them about boundaries. A child who doesn't understand boundaries might not recognize appropriate versus inappropriate behavior, nor can they tell when someone has crossed their boundaries, or they have crossed someone else's. Educate your child on recognizing appropriate interactions and respecting personal space. Predators may exploit a child's affectionate nature by encouraging physical contact in a way that makes the child initiate hugs or touches, blurring the lines of appropriate interaction. Be cautious of adults who frequently have your child sit on their lap, especially if they position the child inappropriately.

Not every adult who does this has bad intentions, but it's a common method predators use to normalize close physical contact. Adults with a healthy mindset typically maintain boundaries and respect the child's comfort with physical closeness, allowing the child to decide if they want to engage in hugs or be picked up. Sometimes, parents unwittingly pressure their children to show affection to relatives or friends; it's important to allow your child to make decisions about their body and to say "no" to unwanted touch, regardless of the person's relation to them. My experiences taught me the importance of not feeling silent and controlling who touches me, lessons I learned too late. Teaching children about personal space and appropriate boundaries should start early, helping them to navigate their relationships with peers and understand the concept of inappropriate touching. This education is crucial in preventing them from being placed in uncomfortable situations.

Education: Starting the conversation about inappropriate touching early ensures that children develop boundaries and safety from a young age. At around three to five years old, children begin to grasp basic concepts and language, an opportune time to introduce simple yet essential ideas about body autonomy and what constitutes appropriate and inappropriate touching. The conversation should be approached in a gentle and age-appropriate manner, using simple terms, and examples that children can understand. Emphasizing concepts like "private parts," "good touch," and "bad touch," and the importance of telling a trusted adult if someone makes them feel uncomfortable can empower children to recognize and respond to potentially harmful situations.

As children grow older, the conversation can evolve to include more detailed information about different types of abuse, the importance of consent, and strategies for seeking help if they ever experience or witness inappropriate behavior. By laying this foundation early on, parents and caregivers equip children with the knowledge and confidence they need to protect themselves and seek support, if necessary, throughout their lives. Additionally, it's crucial to educate teenage girls and boys that they have the right to change their minds or decline any sexual proposition without feeling pressured or obligated to comply. At any point during a sexual encounter, they have the absolute right to reconsider and withdraw consent. This means that even if they initially consented or showed interest, they are not obligated to continue if they feel uncomfortable or no longer wish to participate. Their autonomy and comfort should always be respected and prioritized. It's important to communicate openly and feel empowered to assert their boundaries and preferences, regardless of the stage of the interaction.

I hesitated to share this aspect of my story, but I believe authenticity and raising awareness require honesty. Most of my friends were older than me, so we often spent time together, as a group. When I was approximately 12 years old, a guy in the neighborhood developed an interest in me. He was around 18 years old at the time. As a young girl, I didn't pay much attention to the age difference; I was smitten, much like many girls that age tend to be. It was during this period that I lost my virginity. I was cautious not to give the wrong impression and never mentioned that I was still a virgin; honestly, I'm not sure if he ever questioned or was interested in knowing. I always told the truth about my age; he was fully aware of how old I was. I didn't want to come off as a "tease." I was naive and frightened, unsure if I could refuse because of the situation, I'd put myself in. It wasn't until my daughter turned 12 years old that I observed her lack of maturity and realized she wouldn't be capable of giving consent. It prompted me to reflect on my own experience at that age and recognize that I had the right to stop it. However, due to my tendency to yield to others and my fear of men, I didn't. I had to learn to remember my body, my choice, and my consent matter above all else.

The perception of young girls who engage in sexual relationships or exhibit promiscuous behavior being labeled as *fast* or *loose* is deeply ingrained in many societies and can have damaging effects. This societal judgment often fails to consider the underlying trauma or factors that may have influenced the behavior. These traumatic experiences can lead to emotional distress and a distorted view of relationships and sexuality. Girls and boys who have experienced trauma or adverse childhood experiences may struggle with low self-esteem and seek validation and acceptance through relationships or sexual activity, even if it's harmful to them. There's often a double standard when it comes to views of male and female sexuality, with girls facing greater stigma and judgment for their sexual behavior compared to boys. Instead of recognizing the trauma or underlying issues that may have contributed to their behavior, young girls are often blamed and shamed for their choices, further exacerbating their emotional distress. By understanding and addressing the complex factors that contribute to young girls' involvement in sexual relationships or promiscuous behavior, we can work towards creating more supportive and empowering environments for their well-being and growth.

The age of consent in my hometown is 16 years old. This means that individuals who are 16 years old or older can legally consent to sexual activity with partners who are also 16 years old or older. Laws regarding the age of consent can vary by jurisdiction and may be subject to change, so it's advisable to consult the most current legal statutes.

Community Involvement. Community involvement plays a crucial role in enhancing the safety and well-being of children, acting as a preventive measure against child abuse, including sexual abuse. Reviewing the National Sex Offender Registry is an effective method for determining whether any registered sex offenders reside in your vicinity. By accessing this database, individuals can obtain valuable information regarding the presence of sex offenders who have been convicted of sex offenses within their community. This proactive approach empowers individuals to make informed decisions about their safety and the safety of their loved ones by being aware of potential risks and taking appropriate precautions. Also, active engagement from various community members, organizations, and institutions can create a supportive environment that promotes awareness, education, and action to protect children.

Here are some ways through which community involvement can make a significant impact:

1. Education and Awareness Programs

Communities can organize workshops, seminars, and training sessions for children, parents, educators, and other community members to raise awareness about the signs of child abuse, prevention strategies, and the importance of creating safe spaces for children. Educating the community about grooming tactics, online safety, and boundary-setting can empower individuals to recognize and respond to potential threats.

2. School Involvement

Schools can incorporate curriculum-based programs that teach children about personal safety, consent, body autonomy, and healthy relationships from an early age. Teachers and staff should also be trained to identify signs of abuse and know how to respond appropriately.

3. Neighborhood Watch Programs

Communities can establish neighborhood watch or child watch programs, where trained volunteers watch for suspicious behavior or situations that may put children at risk. These programs can foster a sense of collective responsibility for the safety of all children in the community.

4. Support Networks

Creating support networks for survivors and families affected by child abuse can provide crucial emotional support, legal guidance, and advocacy. These networks can also be instrumental in breaking the silence around abuse and encouraging others to come forward.

5. Collaboration with Local Authorities

Communities can work closely with local law enforcement, social services, and child protection agencies to ensure a coordinated response to incidents of child abuse. This includes reporting mechanisms, investigation processes, and intervention strategies that prioritize the child's well-being.

6. Safe Spaces for Children

Establishing safe spaces within communities, such as youth centers, sports clubs, and after-school programs, where children can engage in activities under the supervision of vetted, trusted adults. These spaces can also offer educational resources and emotional support for children.

7. Public Campaigns and Events

Organizing public campaigns and community events to highlight the importance of child protection can help to keep the issue in the public consciousness, mobilize resources, and galvanize community action.

8. Policy Advocacy

Community groups can advocate for stronger policies, regulations, and resources dedicated to child protection at the local, state, and national levels. This includes pushing for background checks for individuals working with children, mandatory reporting laws, and funding for child protection programs.

Community involvement in child protection requires a multifaceted approach, combining education, vigilance, and support to create an environment where children are safe, valued, and empowered to speak out. Through collective action, communities can significantly reduce the risk of child abuse and ensure that children grow up in safe, nurturing environments.

What to Do if Your Child is a Victim

Children may be hesitant to speak about abuse for various reasons. They might fear repercussions from the abuser, worry about not being believed, feel ashamed or embarrassed, or think that they are somehow to blame for the abuse. Additionally, children may feel pressure to protect the family's reputation or avoid causing distress to their guardians. In some cases, children may not recognize the abusive behavior as wrong or may lack the vocabulary to express what has happened to them. These factors can create significant barriers to disclosure and make it difficult for children to speak up about their experiences of abuse. However, if you sense or believe your child has been a victim, it is your responsibility to create a safe and supportive environment for them to disclose their experiences, seek appropriate help and support, and take necessary steps to ensure their safety and well-being.

One precaution I've taken with my daughter, about which I won't give too many specifics, is establishing a "safe word." Only she and I are privy of this word. I've encouraged her to create her own words with her father. I've explained that if she texts or say the safe word, I'll come to her aid without hesitation. While I may not respond directly, she can count on me to be on my way. In the rare event that I'm unavailable, only if circumstances prevent me from reaching her, she knows the identity of the trusted individual I'll send in my place details we've kept between us.

If you choose to adopt this practice, it's essential to establish clear rules and guidelines and to adhere to them firmly, even if your child misuses the system; simply emphasize to them the significance of reserving the word for genuine emergencies. Additionally, I've introduced another word that she can utilize if the situation requires my attention but isn't urgent. Building trust with your children is paramount. If you discover or suspect your child is a victim of abuse, taking immediate, supportive, and protective actions is critical. Here are steps to consider:

Stay Calm: Your reaction can profoundly impact your child. Showing calmness and support helps them feel safe and understood. Your showing anger towards the abuser could be misconstrued by the child as anger towards them. Remember, children often have a protective instinct and may hesitate to upset you. If they sense you becoming agitated or reacting strongly, they might withdraw their statement.

Believe Your Child: Affirm their feelings and reassure them that it's not their fault. Children rarely lie about abuse, and your belief in them is foundational to their healing. It is not up to you to figure out if your child is deceitful or not. Disregarding any of their feelings may do more harm than good in the long run.

Listen Carefully: Allow your child to share their experience at their own pace without pressing for details. Your role is to listen and validate their feelings. If you're seeking specific information from them, consider asking if they can identify the person responsible, where they were touched, and if they can demonstrate how it happened, if feasible. Inquire whether they've experienced a similar touch from anyone else. Ask about their feelings during the encounter, but always be conscious of the child's comfort and readiness to share.

Seek Medical Attention: If the abuse is recent, a medical exam can be vital for health concerns and evidence collection. Even if the abuse happened in the past, a medical check-up is important for their well-being. Seeking medical attention after experiencing abuse is crucial for several reasons. Firstly, it allows for the immediate assessment and treatment of any physical injuries sustained during the incident. Medical professionals can provide necessary medical care, including treatment for injuries and testing for sexually transmitted infections (STIs). Additionally, seeking medical attention enables the collection of forensic evidence, which can be vital for legal proceedings and holding the perpetrator accountable.

Preserve Evidence: If the abuse is recent, try not to wash clothes or any items the perpetrator might have touched and avoid bathing your child before a medical exam. Preserving evidence after abuse is significant for several reasons. Firstly, it can provide valuable documentation about the abuse, which may be necessary for legal proceedings. Preserved evidence can also help corroborate the victim's account and support their case in court. Additionally, preserving evidence can aid law enforcement agencies in identifying and apprehending the perpetrator, preventing further harm to the victim or others.

Report the Abuse: If you discover the perpetrator is someone you know, refrain from contacting them, and prioritize your and your child's safety. In case of immediate danger, call 911. Reach out to your state's Child Protective Services. Additionally, you can contact the National Sexual Assault Hotline at 800-656-HOPE (4673) to speak with a trained professional from your local sexual assault service provider who can help. You may also contact your local Child Advocacy Center.

Seek Professional Help: Counseling by a therapist specializing in child abuse can provide your child and your family with the necessary support to navigate through the healing process.

Educate Yourself and Your Child: Learn about the impacts of abuse and strategies for healing. Help your child develop coping skills and encourage open communication about feelings and fears, as this can empower them to navigate the healing process with resilience and strength. By educating yourself about the impacts of abuse and strategies for healing, you can provide informed support and guidance to your child as they recover from the trauma. Remember to prioritize their emotional well-being and create a safe and nurturing environment where they feel valued, heard, and supported. Together, you can embark on a journey towards healing and restoration, fostering hope and resilience.

Create a Supportive Environment: Ensure the child is surrounded by a loving and understanding community; support from family, friends, and possibly support groups can be invaluable. Creating a supportive environment after a child has been a victim of abuse is essential for their emotional healing, rebuilding trust, empowerment, normalization of experiences, prevention of re-traumatization, access to resources, and long-term recovery.

Maintain Routine and Stability: Keeping a routine can provide a sense of normalcy and security for the child amidst the turmoil. Routine provides a sense of predictability and security, which can help alleviate anxiety and promote feelings of safety for the child. Consistent daily routines, such as regular mealtimes, bedtime rituals, and structured activities, provide stability during uncertainty and upheaval. Consistent routines promote healthy habits, such as regular sleep patterns, balanced nutrition, and physical activity, which is essential for their physical and emotional health. Stability in their daily lives also fosters opportunities for growth, and social interaction, contributing to their cognitive, social, and emotional development.

Legal Advice: Consider consulting a lawyer who specializes in child abuse cases to understand your rights and options for legal action against the perpetrator.

Protect Your Child's Privacy: Share information only with individuals who need to know, like professionals helping your family. This protects your child from additional stress or trauma.

Encourage Your Child: Encourage them to express their feelings and make choices where appropriate, helping them regain a sense of control over their life, rebuild their self-esteem, and develop resilience. Encouraging your child provides the tools and confidence to speak up about their experiences, set boundaries, and seek help when needed. This empowerment process fosters their healing journey, promotes their emotional well-being, and equips them with the skills to navigate future challenges with strength and resilience.

Be Patient: Healing from abuse is a long-term process. Your child may have ups and downs. Continuous support and understanding are crucial throughout their recovery journey. Patience allows the child to feel safe and supported as they navigate their emotions and experiences. It enables them to open up at their own pace, express their feelings without fear of judgment, and gradually rebuild trust in themselves and others. By being patient, caregivers create a nurturing environment where the child feels valued and understood, fostering their emotional healing and resilience. This patience also demonstrates unconditional love and support.

Sexual abuse can profoundly impact the mental health of an entire family. While seeking therapy is a natural step toward healing, it's necessary to prioritize support for the child who has endured the violation, as this traumatic event can significantly affect their mental stability. However, therapy alone may not be sufficient, especially if the family is not financially able to access it. It's important to explore alternative forms of support and intervention. This could include seeking assistance from community organizations, support groups, or religious institutions that offer free or low-cost counseling services. Additionally, involving trusted family members, friends, or teachers who can provide emotional support and understanding can be beneficial.

Moreover, the Black community is reluctant to seek counseling because there's a prevalent lack of trust in the system, stemming from a history of mistreatment and misdiagnosis. Despite the challenges our families faced in accessing therapy in the past, there is a growing trend of adults seeking therapists for themselves and their kids within the community. Nevertheless, the decisions made in response to a child's traumatic experience profoundly influence their healing process and their future well-being. I believe that if I had undergone therapy in my youth and felt protected and listened to, it could have not only fostered trust between my parents and me but also facilitated my transition from childhood to adulthood by enabling me to develop healthier and more satisfying relationships with peers, romantic partners, and family members.

Important Contacts and Resources

Immediate Assistance
Emergency Services:

- Dial **911** for immediate help in emergencies.

Specialized Support
National Sexual Assault Hotline:

- 1-800-656-HOPE (4673)
- Confidential 24/7 support, free resources.

National Child Abuse Hotline:

- 1-800-4-A-CHILD (1-800-422-4453)
- Available 24/7, it offers crisis intervention, information, and referrals to emergency, social service, and support resources.

Domestic Violence Hotline:

- 1-800-799-SAFE (7233)
- 24-hour support for anyone facing domestic violence.

Mental Health Support
National Suicide Prevention Lifeline:

- 1-800-273-TALK (1-800-273-8255)
- 24/7, free and confidential support for people in distress.

Crisis Text Line:

- Text HELLO to 741741
- Free, 24/7 support for those in crisis via text message.

Remember, you are not alone. Help is available, and it's okay to reach out.

CHAPTER THREE

Patterns Unravel

Seeking Love in the Wrong Places

Seeking love in the wrong places refers to attempting to find emotional fulfillment and connection in environments or relationships that are unlikely to provide genuine, healthy, or lasting love. When childhood trauma remains unresolved, it often manifests in various characteristics and behaviors that persist into adulthood. These may include difficulty regulating emotions, feelings of worthlessness, inadequacy, or self-blame, the tendency to avoid situations, people, or places that trigger memories of past trauma, difficulty trusting others, people pleasing, engaging in destructive behaviors, struggling to assert boundaries, and difficulty forming secure attachments or maintain healthy relationships.

Recognizing and addressing childhood trauma is essential for personal growth and healing in adulthood. The first step is acknowledging the existence of your inner child and the pain it holds. Inner child wounds refer to emotional or psychological injuries that individuals carry from their childhood experiences. These wounds are often deep-seated and can profoundly impact a person's thoughts, feelings, and behaviors in adulthood. Validating that your feelings, fears, and reactions may stem from past wounds that need attention; consequently, understanding the impact they have on your adult life and actively working towards healing.

The facade I wore served as my solace. Externally, I presented myself as composed, frequently wearing a bright smile. I excelled in projecting happiness. Concealed beneath it all was a fractured core, unknown to anyone but me, the hidden reality of a wounded child. This world is filled with countless broken adults. Instead of nurturing myself with love, I poured it all into everyone else around me. Boundaries were non-existent; I wanted to fulfill every need for everyone. In the process, I taught them how to use me. Saying "no" was out of the question, overridden by guilt that constantly taunted me. I justified canceling plans to make myself available for everyone, convinced myself to lend money, and brushed off any concerns about repayment.

Succumbing to guilt became second nature. I realized I had been functioning as an enabler, always striving to fulfill everyone's needs. It was a revelation to see how my availability appeared to determine my value in their eyes; when I stopped being constantly available, I noticed a shift in how I was treated. While I might have been the favorite friend, granddaughter, cousin, or niece when I was at everyone's beck and call, the same people wouldn't bother to check in on me when I pulled back. Instead, they would express resentment and criticize my absence.

The fear of rejection weighed heavily on me, so I continued to make myself constantly available. When I wasn't, I was met with guilt trips and pressure to show up, mostly internally. A person who struggles with inner child wounds tends to be a people pleaser. This behavior might stem from fear of rejection and a desire to satisfy their ego. However, there's more to people-pleasing behavior than merely fear of rejection, a subtle yet persistent sense of ego gratification also fuels it. The praise and admiration garnered from fulfilling others' needs provided a temporary boost to my self-esteem, momentarily filling the void left by my unresolved inner wounds. This validation served to mask or alleviate the underlying feelings of inadequacy and insecurity. However, because others' perceptions and expectations determined the validation, it remained momentary and did not address the root causes of my inner struggles. Many people are reluctant to acknowledge this aspect of people-pleasing, perhaps due to discomfort or a lack of readiness to confront it; personally, it took me some time to come to terms with this side of the behavior.

Unhealed trauma can manifest in the workplace in various ways. For instance, you might take on someone else's responsibilities. You might even take the blame for others' mistakes without voicing your opinions or concerns. This was a pattern I fell into frequently. Whenever problems occur, I would simply fix them, instead of involving everyone in the office. My mindset was, "If there's a problem, just fix it there's no need to assign blame."

Over time, I realized the importance of speaking up and reciprocating the actions I received from others. I mostly kept to myself, preferring the solitude of my office. Being highly intuitive, and able to sense other's energy, this heightened awareness often led me to avoid certain individuals or carefully manage my interactions with them. Learning to set boundaries and communicate effectively has been essential in breaking these patterns and ensuring a healthier work environment for myself.

People are drawn to the version of me that looked past their flaws, supported them, listened without judgment, and consistently provided help when needed. Although it seldom came back my way. Living by the principle of treating others as I wished to be treated, I extended the kindness and understanding I yearned for myself.

While there was a degree of self-gratification, I recognize that many actions are driven by immediate personal satisfaction. Yet, I felt that serving others aligns with my spiritual calling, and my efforts were always heartfelt. It's important to me that the genuine intentions of my heart aren't overshadowed.

Some individuals may use relationships to cope with unresolved trauma or emotional pain. Seeking love or validation from others can temporarily distract you from internal distress, but it ultimately perpetuates a cycle of seeking external sources of validation. Individuals who endure childhood trauma often seek love in the wrong places due to various psychological factors stemming from their early experiences. Childhood trauma can shape our beliefs about ourselves, others, and love itself. If you experienced neglect, abuse, or abandonment during your formative years, you may internalize messages that you are unworthy of love or that love is conditional and comes with pain.

As a result, you may be drawn to relationships that confirm these beliefs, perpetuating a cycle of seeking love in places that ultimately reinforce your trauma. People tend to recreate familiar relationship dynamics from childhood, even if those dynamics are unhealthy or abusive. Abuse, whether emotional, physical, or sexual, introduces a toxic association between love and pain. For someone who grew up in an environment where love is expressed through harmful actions or is accompanied by abuse, it becomes difficult to dissociate affection from suffering. This skewed perception can make it challenging to form healthy relationships, as the individual may unconsciously expect or accept harmful behaviors as a part of being loved. When you're still struggling with unresolved issues, you tend to gravitate towards men or women who are emotionally distant or have unresolved childhood traumas, as well.

Be cautious about how much you reveal concerning your past and the trauma you've experienced. If possible, avoid showing that you lack family support. When someone realizes you have no support system except for them, a manipulative person might exploit that vulnerability to mistreat you. They may isolate you and have you solely dependent on them; they may feel empowered to use this as leverage to treat you poorly. This situation can create a power imbalance, where the dependent person is more vulnerable, and the other person may exploit this position to manipulate or control them. Being aware of such dynamics, by sharing too much, you risk not only being controlled but also potentially facing physical, emotional, and verbal abuse.

A person who needs to control others often exhibits a strong desire to dictate the behavior, decisions, and actions of people around them. This need for control typically stems from deeper issues such as insecurity, fear of unpredictability, or past traumas that have left them feeling powerless or vulnerable. Such individuals may use various tactics like manipulation, coercion, or authority to maintain a sense of security or superiority. They might try to seem strong or put together, but their actions reveal the truth. A manipulative person is adept at detecting low self-esteem, often because they can empathize as well. However, instead of using this insight to encourage you, they manipulate it for their benefit, exploiting your vulnerabilities to serve their interests rather than helping you.

Subconsciously, people seek out partners who resemble their parents/caregivers, hoping to resolve past issues or gain the love and validation they lacked as children. Reflecting on my past, I realize that I never pursued relationships with emotionally available men. I saw men who were affectionate as too clingy. It simply didn't sit well with me. Reciprocating that kind of affection was beyond my comfort zone; I didn't know how to handle it. Instead, I sabotaged those relationships, acting emotionlessly towards them. The more they showed care and effort, the more I withdrew. I would distance myself to protect these men from being hurt by my actions. However, when they persisted and continued pursuing me, I often responded by ghosting them.

During my early years, I often found myself involved with toxic guys. They would try to manipulate me, attempting to undermine my confidence. I encountered men who blatantly said that no one genuinely desired me and that I was merely being used. This disconnect left me puzzled. If I'm truly not a good person, why were they trying to hold on to me? I've had men declare that they wouldn't allow anyone else to have me. I pleaded with them to just leave me alone. I've encountered situations where men would stalk me, finding them lurking in bushes or beneath cars, lingering on nearby street corners. It was a terrifying ordeal.

I was a victim of date rape. Date rape refers to a form of sexual assault where the perpetrator and the victim have a pre-existing relationship, which can range from acquaintanceship to a romantic or sexual relationship. The term "date rape" emphasizes that the assault occurs within the context of a social or dating situation, but it's important to note that the core issue is the lack of consent from the victim, regardless of their relationship with the assailant. We often overlook the experiences of women who have endured assault by the men they are in a relationship with or are dating.

I met my husband, Jay, during our high school years. We initiated a romantic relationship at the age of seventeen. Before we were married, we experienced a temporary separation in our early twenties. It was during this period that I started dating a man who, for this book, I will call Kendrick.

Kendrick and I had only been dating for about three or four months after parting ways with Jay. Kendrick invited me out to dinner, a common occurrence since we typically saw each other or communicated a few times a week. Although we hung out on multiple occasions, I wasn't comfortable becoming intimate with him.

After dinner, he suggested we go to a party at a hotel. This seemed normal enough, as my friends and I often attended hotel parties. On the way, he mentioned he needed to stop by his house to pick up something. When he came out of the house, he was carrying a black bag, which I was already aware of what he kept in it, a pistol for protection, which didn't alarm me given the circumstances. However, rather than going directly to the hotel, he made a stop at a nearby restaurant to use the restroom. The restaurant was conveniently located in the same parking lot as the hotel. I didn't dwell on it much, assuming he chose the restaurant's restroom because he anticipated the hotel room would be crowded. However, later, I assumed that might not have been the case. I wasn't focusing on the direction he took because I was texting on my phone. This highlights the importance of being aware of your surroundings.

When he returned to the car, we drove around to the hotel, but I noticed the parking lot was unusually empty. I questioned the lack of cars, and he brushed it off, claiming we were early. As we approached the entrance, he took out a set of keys and admitted that the room was just for us. I immediately felt uneasy and asked to be taken home. Ignoring my request, he unlocked the door and pulled me inside, where he placed his bag on one of the double beds. I sat on the edge of the other bed, repeatedly asking him to drive me home. At that moment, my ex-boyfriend, Jay, called. When he saw who was calling, he grabbed the phone from my hand. He grew increasingly upset, repeatedly claiming that my lingering feelings for Jay were the reason I wouldn't give him a chance.

I insisted that I simply wasn't ready and repeatedly asked to be taken home. Despite my pleas, he refused to return my phone or take me home.

He started begging me to be intimate with him, insisting that we both wanted it, but I continued to say, "No, I don't." I wrestled with him to try to prevent him from pushing me back onto the bed. As he began to remove my clothes, I tried to resist. Then, he glanced at the bed, and at that moment, I stopped resisting. I realized I needed to make it home to my mom. I was terrified. I lay there, teary-eyed, but he didn't stop. He proceeded to violate me. I did not put up a fight at this point. I surrendered. He wore no protection. After he finished, he got up, and we departed. I was speechless. I couldn't believe what had just occurred. When I arrived home, I didn't tell anyone. I went directly to the bathtub and sat there without shedding a tear, simply sitting there in disbelief.

To add insult to injury, this guy worked in upholstery, and he was currently reupholstering my mom's furniture. It was a bad situation to be in. My relationship with my mom was already strained, and she was asking when she would get her furniture back. I had no desire to talk to this man, but I knew I had to reclaim her furniture. I finally mustered up the nerve to reach out to him. I inquired about when he planned to return the furniture, and his response was, "Is there something you need to tell me?" To my surprise, he assumed I was calling to announce I was pregnant.

In my experience, the boundaries of consent were crossed, leaving me feeling deeply violated and traumatized. Women have the right to say no at any point; your body is yours, regardless of circumstances or feelings. Even if you felt aroused at some point, it's okay to set boundaries and change your mind. No one deserves to experience betrayal in that manner. It's important to understand that no one ever deserves or asks to be raped, regardless of their relationship with the person or any previous interactions. This type of assault can have profound and long-lasting effects on victims, affecting their mental health, relationships, and sense of safety and trust. It's important to recognize and acknowledge the seriousness of date rape and provide support and resources to victims as they navigate their healing journey.

Since the attention I always received tended to be negative, I believed that covering up or speaking negatively about myself would deter further attention. I made considerable efforts to avoid attention. I wore loose-fitting clothes and adopted a tomboyish style. Due to experiencing multiple instances of sexual assault by different men, I developed an intense fear of men. Even while dating, I had mastered concealing my fear, never allowing anyone to witness my anxiety or trepidation, despite feeling terrified in many instances. While I continued to date, I struggled to assert my right to say "no." I often blamed myself for the situations, so felt obligated to comply with their demands.

Consequently, I remained in some "situationships" not because I felt loved and cared for, but I perceived them as safe and protective since they never tried to take advantage of me. I placed my trust in these men without considering how they treated me. Separate from some who have gone through sexual assault and turned to promiscuous behavior, I couldn't bring myself to do the same.

The tendency to choose emotionally unavailable partners often stems from childhood experiences of feeling rejected or emotionally neglected by primary caregivers. This can create a deep-seated belief that one is inherently unworthy or inadequate, leading to a subconscious desire to prove one's worthiness by breaking down the emotional barriers of others. The individual may believe that if they can show just enough love, attention, or kindness to their partner, they will finally feel validated and complete. This pattern is driven by a longing to fill the void left by past emotional wounds and a subconscious belief that validation from others will heal these inner hurts. Some individuals yearn for love, understanding, and validation, but it's important to realize that these desires must first be found within yourself. Self-love, grace, and acceptance are foundational before seeking them externally. It's important to acknowledge that nobody owes you these things, as often the individuals from whom you seek them may be unable to provide them due to their emotional wounds.

Many people carry deeply rooted traumas, and sometimes we are drawn to others through a process known as trauma bond. This bond forms when two individuals develop a profound, yet unhealthy emotional attachment rooted in shared trauma. Such relationships often cycle between periods of abuse, love bombing, and kindness. The term, "love bombing" means bombarding someone with love, often at an overwhelming rate and intensity. While love bombing may initially feel flattering and exciting, it is ultimately a form of emotional manipulation and control. The individual may use love bombing to establish a sense of power and control over you, making it difficult for you to assert your boundaries or recognize red flags in the relationship.

As the relationship progresses, the love bomber may gradually withdraw their affection or become increasingly demanding, leading to feelings of confusion, insecurity, and emotional instability. Initially, the person may shower you with affection and gifts, fostering a sense of attachment. These dynamics can occur in various relationships where the individual may intermittently display kindness, leading you to hold onto hope for a return to those moments of affection. They might go weeks without communicating with you, only to suddenly reach out and express how much they miss you or even profess their love for you. Their goal is to keep you trapped in a never-ending cycle. They merely want to maintain access to you. It's crucial to exercise caution in these situations because individuals in this dynamic are emotionally unstable and may react poorly to rejection if you attempt to leave. They are capable of and may resort to causing physical harm.

There are alternative pathways through which individuals can enter our lives, guided by divine influence, without necessarily leading to toxicity. While I won't delve into the numerous types of connections, I firmly believe in the reality of soul connections. Soul connections come in various forms and don't always have to be toxic or negative. These connections can be divinely guided and serve as sources of love, support, and growth in your life. Whether it's a divine connection orchestrated by a higher power, these connections can manifest in friendships, mentorships, or even chance encounters with strangers.

Soul connections surpass conventional categories and are characterized by a deep sense of understanding, resonance, and mutual respect between individuals. These relationships have the potential to bring immense joy, fulfillment, and spiritual evolution. Meeting someone on a soul level can feel like encountering an old friend or kindred spirit, even if you've just met. These connections can serve as sparks for personal growth, and spiritual awakening, or provide comfort and support during challenging times. Whether it's a brief encounter or a lifelong friendship, these connections remind us of the interconnectedness of all beings and the profound beauty of human connection beyond the superficial. It's important to discern the nature of the connections we form and recognize when a relationship is not healthy or serving us.

Walking away from toxic relationships is an important act of self-love and self-preservation. Instead of dwelling on what you believe you're losing, concentrate on the benefits of releasing a toxic person from your life. Understand that this allows for personal growth and assures that the best is still ahead. By honoring your boundaries and prioritizing your well-being, you create space for healthier, more authentic connections to enter your life. Perceive which type of connection you're experiencing and recognize that any relationship detrimental to your mental and physical health should be gracefully exited.

I presented myself as though I required nothing from anyone, no support, no love, or the need for anyone to understand me. Yet deep down, I felt the complete opposite. The fear of rejection loomed large within me. In relationships, I found myself at odds with my feelings; part of me craved love, yet the fear of being dominated, manipulated, and rejected led me to conceal my genuine wants and desires. To others, I portrayed myself as the quintessential "homegirl."

In many previous connections, I often felt like the fallback option - the person they would turn to when convenient, but not necessarily the one they were fully committed to. I was the confidante, the one they sought out for support and encouragement, the one they felt safe to share their secrets and inner thoughts with, yet I was often perceived as too challenging. I held them accountable for their actions most of the time or voiced my opinion when they were involved in questionable behavior. I recognize the importance of taking responsibility for my actions including what I permitted and endured. By condoning their behavior towards me, I inadvertently discourage any incentive for change. It required me to acknowledge that some men may not be ready for change, or I was never the one; navigating this can be emotionally draining.

Interestingly, some emotionally unavailable men are drawn to the *homegirl* characteristic of women. However, they may also harbor a sense of distrust towards it concurrently. While some saw me as a "good woman" with potential, they were reluctant to commit to me fully. Although they didn't want to see me with anyone else, they weren't ready to be emotionally vulnerable to me; embracing this role as the "backburner girl" allowed me to avoid being emotionally present. I had a deep fear of vulnerability. I prioritize protecting myself from potential emotional hurt by not fully engaging or investing in the relationship emotionally.

Naturally, one can yearn for love and companionship while struggling with emotional availability. This often arises from unresolved issues or past traumas that hinder their ability to engage deeply in intimate relationships. While I longed for love and connection on a surface level, I found it challenging to be emotionally vulnerable or sustain profound, meaningful bonds. Consequently, I fell into a pattern of pursuing relationships without wholeheartedly emotionally investing. Although I could fully commit, I encountered difficulty in engaging emotionally.

People opt for relationships or friendships with others who are also struggling because it allows them to avoid confronting their behaviors. This was certainly true in my experience; not having to be fully invested emotionally allowed me to maintain a level of detachment. It acted as a protective barrier, safeguarding me from the openness and deep emotional engagement that true intimacy requires. Over time, however, I recognized that this detachment also kept me from experiencing the full depth of genuine connections and personal growth. It became clear that by not showing up emotionally, I was not only limiting my relationship but also my emotional development.

Looking back on my relationship spanning more than 25 years, it's apparent that despite Jay fulfilling the role of a provider, there was a significant emotional gap. While he consistently offered financial support and was present during times of my sickness, the underlying absence of emotional connection left me feeling unfulfilled and neglected. What I came to understand about my relationship was that while the financial and sexual aspects were present, it was the "everything in between" that was lacking. The "everything in between" in a relationship refers to emotional intimacy, communication, shared interests, mutual support, and overall connection beyond the financial and sexual aspects. It encompasses the day-to-day interactions, the quality time spent together, the emotional support given during difficult times, and the shared experiences, goals, and values that strengthen the bond between partners. Essentially, it's the substance of the relationship that goes beyond the surface-level aspects and contributes to its depth and longevity.

I'm not diminishing his contribution as a provider, because he excelled in that role. I recognize the obstacles and socio-economic hurdles men encounter in fulfilling their duties, along with the immense pressure they bear. Also, other factors such as stress, feelings of not being enough, past trauma, and mental health challenges they may have endured. I would never disregard that aspect; I hold deep appreciation for him in that regard.

The relationship fostered a sense of inadequacy, as though I was perpetually relegated to the back burner while other things took precedence. Despite assurances from others that he was a "good man," I struggled with the notion that financial stability alone could not compensate for the emotional void felt. In my family, there's a prevailing teaching that good men are those who can provide. This concept extends beyond supplying my material needs; it encompasses emotional support, stability, and the strength to uplift and protect the family. There was infidelity within the relationship, which acted as a channel, reopening old wounds of inadequacy and reinforcing the belief that I was not enough. Infidelity didn't significantly contribute to the disconnect; it was the absence of changed behavior and reassurance that ultimately strained the relationship. My pleas for emotional connection went unanswered, as he seemed incapable or unwilling to meet me on that level. It became apparent that resentment on his behalf lingered beneath the surface, derived from perceived pressures regarding marriage after a decade-long relationship.

Even with my efforts to bridge the emotional gap, our interactions were influenced by this unresolved tension, leaving me scrambling with a profound, pervasive sense of unmet needs. The emotional strain became particularly evident as I went through the experiences of 3 miscarriages before conceiving our daughter. These losses deeply affected my mental health, leaving me feeling devoid of support and disconnected from others. This isolation weighed heavily on me and exacerbated tensions within my marriage.

Additionally, it shook my faith as I struggled to reconcile these losses with my beliefs. I resisted the idea of having children due to my fear of being unable to protect them. Despite assisting in raising other family members' and friends' children, including my Godchildren, I was apprehensive about assuming sole responsibility. Although I faced criticism for my reluctance to have children and felt pressured to justify myself, I was embarrassed by my underlying reasons. Revealing my fears would have meant exposing a deep personal secret.

The news of my first pregnancy initially left me uncertain. I even asked the nurse to conduct another test, which I dropped on the floor in doubt. It felt like a punishment, and in the face of my attempts to find happiness, I struggled internally. I was questioning why God would give me a child when I doubted my ability to care for him or her. Despite not actively taking preventative measures, I had assumed I couldn't conceive due to my diagnosis of stage 4 endometriosis. Endometriosis is a chronic condition where tissue similar to the lining inside the uterus, known as the endometrium, begins to grow outside the uterus. This misplaced tissue can be found on the ovaries, fallopian tubes, the outer surface of the uterus, and other organs within the pelvis. Endometriosis is known for causing pain, especially during menstrual periods, though its severity can vary.

Other symptoms may include heavy periods, pain during intercourse, infertility, and discomfort during bowel movements or urination. The exact cause of endometriosis is not known, but it is believed to involve a combination of genetic, hormonal, and immune system factors. Endometriosis is categorized into four stages, ranging from stage one, the least severe, to stage four, the most severe. These stages are determined by the severity, location, and size of the endometrial implants. Endometriosis had severely affected my daily life, leaving me in constant pain, with some days being so unbearable that I couldn't gain the strength to get out of bed. This further contributed to the difficulties within our marriage because there were days when I couldn't fulfill my role as his wife.

Following the first loss in an ectopic pregnancy, my determination to have a child intensified. However, two subsequent pregnancies ended in further disappointment. My mental health suffered, and I battled periods of depression. I struggled to comprehend why I had to endure such traumatic experiences. I needed Jay's presence and support during these challenging periods. However, it seems that some men lack a true understanding of the deep impact miscarriages have on women. They fail to comprehend the emotional bond we form and the nurturing instinct that arises instantly when a woman discovers she is pregnant. While I believe he genuinely cared for me and was sad to witness my pain, he struggled to find the right words to comfort me. He was sincerely apologetic, yet unable to provide the encouragement I needed.

I must also recognize my role. It's unfair to attribute all the blame to him for the emotional immaturity in our relationship, as my past trauma made it difficult for me to fully engage. Although I didn't refrain from sexual intimacy with him, despite experiencing pain, I found it challenging to participate in other types of physical closeness and affection. This wasn't deliberate; rather, I simply did not know how to express it. It felt awkward and unfamiliar to me, as well.

Additionally, years of infidelity created a barrier, making me hesitant to let him in emotionally. I would at times opt for silence instead of expressing my needs openly. I would retreat behind the protective walls I had built internally and disconnect from the connection. It may go unnoticed by many, but depending on its application, silence can be a means of manipulation within a relationship. Using silence, such as needing time to process information or emotions, choosing not to engage in conflict, or simply not having anything to say, is not manipulative. However, silence can become manipulative when used as a tactic to control or manipulate others, such as withholding communication to punish or manipulate someone, using silence as a form of passive- aggression, or refusing to communicate to avoid accountability or responsibility. We must be cautious of how we utilize it. I was aware of how it would be used at times.

Withholding sex in a relationship can be seen as a form of manipulation, as well, if it's used intentionally to control or influence the other person's behavior. In relationships, sex can be important aspect of intimacy and connection. Sex can be used as a leverage point and can lead to feelings of confusion, rejection, or inadequacy. However, it's also important to recognize that individuals have the right to consent to or decline sex based on their feelings, health, and comfort levels. It becomes manipulative when the refusal is specifically intended as a tool to exert power or control in the relationship. In healthy relationships, communication about sexual needs, desires and boundaries should be open and respectful, allowing both partners to feel safe and validated.

Knowingly, I tried to exert myself to be there for him to the extent of my comfort level; the initial periods of betrayal, dishonesty, and deception eroded my ability to trust him completely with my heart. I felt isolated, lacking anyone I could genuinely rely on for emotional or mental support. After years of striving to find love within my relationship, I initiated coping mechanisms that proved unbreakable. Despite my pleas for companionship, I was engulfed by an overwhelming sense of emptiness. Ultimately, I remained numb, unable to break free from the walls I had constructed. Deep down, I always doubted whether I was ever truly loved in the way I needed, not just in my marriage but in any relationship.

This lingering doubt cast a shadow over my connections, making me question the authenticity and depth of the affection I received. It wasn't just about hearing the words or witnessing the actions, it was about feeling seen, understood, and cherished for who I was. This desire for a deeper, more meaningful love left me feeling alone, even when surrounded by people who claimed to care for me. I was merely existing, letting life carry me along. I felt increasingly numb, longing to feel something, anything; I had resigned myself to the reality of our relationship, accepting it would never evolve beyond its current state. We were both settled into complacency: there was no abuse, either physical or verbal, so we found a certain comfort in our routine. Nevertheless, neither of us could confess our unhappiness, but I needed more.

After years of merely existing, I discovered myself in a state of vulnerability, though I would never acknowledge it openly. During this period, I began to develop a friendship with a man; for this book, I'll refer to him as "Saunders". This connection opened my eyes to how much more I desired and needed from life. It wasn't specifically about this newfound friendship, but rather the depth and nature of our interactions that proved enlightening.

There was no expectation for this friendship to evolve into something more. However, for the first time, I could be my authentic self without fear of judgment; a stark contrast to what I was used to. I found myself becoming codependent on Saunders. While he, too, was emotionally unavailable, there was a deeper connection between us that we couldn't quite grasp. We shared similar experiences and felt a sense of familiarity. In the face of this, I was drawn to him, seeking comfort in his presence. He understood me. He understood my views. I could freely discuss my religious beliefs and engage in deep conversations about life and my struggle to connect with my emotions.

It was him who I told about the sexual assaults I endured. I didn't confess to him simply because I felt ready to share; rather, he seemed to notice something in my behavior that prompted him to ask me about it directly. At first, I attempted to deny it. He assured me of my safety, but I never delved into the details with him; I had kept this information from everyone in my family, my husband included. While our communication was open, there were still aspects of myself that I opted to conceal from him. However, admitting to him that I had been sexually abused initially felt like a burden lifted.

There was an incident that occurred that incited a reaction from me. This resulted in a shift in my behavior and our connection. Despite this, I still harbored expectations of him being that he opened this safe space, and when he couldn't meet them, I felt rejected, abandoned, and disappointed. It was easier for him when I was emotionally numb and showed no emotions, but when I started having expectations, his avoidance made him withdraw. It was a blow to my ego.

Beyond the ego, being rejected tapped into deeper fears and insecurities I didn't even know I had. My failure to disclose my trauma over the years and my tendency to mask it left me unaware of its true impact. I believe my actions also started triggering him and considering his past, he felt overwhelmed. Even though he opened a safe space, I remembered him telling me, "I didn't sign up for this." At that moment, I should have ended the friendship. If you don't heal underlying wounds, you'll continue encountering the same traits in everyone you meet.

Occasionally, our egos can lead us astray, especially when we face rejection. It becomes evident when we become consumed with winning over the person who rejected us. When a woman experiences rejection, she often feels compelled to invest more in soothing her emotions or ego. This behavior often stems from a lack of understanding of healthy love or a history of competing for affection. Additionally, there is a misconception associating the intensity of romance with the level of suffering endured. This perspective is exacerbated by cultural narratives that glorify the belief in achieving love through relentless pursuit, sometimes neglecting the significance of mutual respect. It highlights the need to educate individuals about identifying and fostering healthy, mutually reciprocal relationships.

However, when faced with rejection, it's not the moment to prove your worthiness; it's time to walk away from the situation. If you don't leave at that point, gaslighting and manipulation are likely to follow, particularly for individuals with abandonment wounds. Gaslighting is a form of psychological manipulation where one person seeks to make another person doubt their perception, memory, or reality. This can manifest in various ways, such as denying something happened, minimizing the other person's feelings, or shifting blame onto them. For someone with abandonment wounds, the fear of being left or rejected can be deeply ingrained, often stemming from past experiences of abandonment or emotional neglect. As a result, they may be more likely to tolerate mistreatment in relationships to avoid being discarded. This can create a cycle where they stay in unhealthy or abusive situations, hoping to prove their worthiness or cling to any semblance of connection, even if it's harmful to them.

Yes, I acknowledge that there was an instance of infidelity on my part, as well, because I developed an emotional dependence on another person. I longed for someone who could be there for me, yet I struggled to find that support. However, it was through this friendship that I began to recognize I had attachment issues. My therapist recommended a book aimed at addressing attachment styles. The book and her guidance taught me my attachment style is disorganized attachment. Individuals with disorganized attachment may exhibit a mix of anxious and avoidant tendencies. My approach to relationships was filled with confusion and contradictory behaviors.

On the one hand, I deeply craved closeness and emotional security from my partners; however, on the other, I found myself feeling trapped or suffocated when closeness became too intense. This push-and-pull dynamic made it difficult for anyone to take me seriously in relationships. My reactions could be unpredictable; moments of intense connection were swiftly followed by periods of withdrawal, driven by an underlying fear of abandonment or rejection. This disorganized way of relating stemmed from earlier experiences that failed to teach me how to form healthy, secure attachments; it manifested in a constant struggle to trust not only the intentions of others but also my feelings.

There are various types of attachment styles that individuals may experience in their relationships: Secure, Anxious-Preoccupied, Dismissive-Avoidant, and Fearful-Avoidant (Disorganized) attachments. Attachment styles can influence how people perceive themselves and others and navigate intimacy, conflict, and emotional connection. Childhood trauma can have a significant impact on the development of attachment styles and patterns in adulthood.

Here's how:

1. **Secure Attachment:** Individuals with a secure attachment style feel comfortable with emotional intimacy and can trust and depend on their partners. They are generally confident in themselves and their relationships.

2. **Anxious-Preoccupied Attachment:** People with an anxious-preoccupied attachment style often worry about their partner's love and may fear rejection or abandonment. They may seek constant reassurance and approval from their partners.

3. **Dismissive-Avoidant Attachment:** Individuals with a dismissive-avoidant attachment style tend to avoid emotional closeness and may appear emotionally distant or detached from their partners. They prioritize independence and may struggle with intimacy.

4. **Fearful-Avoidant (Disorganized):** Those with a fearful- avoidant (disorganized) attachment style has conflicting desires for closeness and independence. They may fear rejection but also feel uncomfortable with emotional intimacy, leading to ambivalence in relationships.

There are several quizzes, books, and questionnaires available to help you discover your attachment style. I've created a simplified version to provide you with an overview of the types of questions that are associated with attachment theory. Keep in mind that this quiz is simplified and may not capture the full complexity of attachment styles. For a more accurate assessment, you may benefit from a professional evaluation or more in-depth questionnaires. It's important to remember that attachment styles are not fixed and can change over time or in different relationships. If you're interested in exploring your attachment style further or seeking support for relationship issues, consider speaking with a therapist or counselor who can provide personalized guidance and insights.

Attachment Style Quiz

1. When it comes to relationships, I feel:
   a) Comfortable and secure;
   b) Anxious and worried about being rejected;
   c) Uncomfortable with emotional intimacy and tend to keep my distance;
   d) Unsure and conflicted, with mixed feelings about closeness and independence.

2. I prefer my partner to:
   a) Provide support and understanding;
   b) Reassure me frequently of their love and commitment;
   c) Give me space and independence;
   d) Respect my need for both closeness and distance.

3. When faced with relationship conflicts, I tend to:
   a) Communicate openly and work towards resolution;
   b) Become anxious and fear abandonment;
   c) Withdraw emotionally or avoid addressing the issue;
   d) Feel overwhelmed and unsure how to respond.

4. My attitude towards commitment is:
    a) Positive, I value commitment and am comfortable with it.
    b) Ambivalent, and I desire commitment but worry about being hurt.
    c) Reluctant, I prefer to keep my options open.
    d) Conflicted, I want commitment but also fear losing my independence.

5. My childhood experiences with caregivers were:
    a) Loving and supportive.
    b) Inconsistent, with periods of both warmth and neglect.
    c) Distant or emotionally unavailable.
    d) Chaotic or abusive.

6. When my partner needs space or time alone, I:
    a) Respect their need for space and give them the room they require.
    b) Feel anxious and worried that they are pulling away from me.
    c) Feel relieved and enjoy having time to myself as well.
    d) Feel uncertain about what their need for space means for our relationship.

7. My reaction to intimacy and physical closeness with my partner is:
    a) Enjoyment and comfort, feeling emotionally connected.
    b) Anxiety and a need for constant reassurance.
    c) Discomfort or a desire to maintain distance.
    d) A mixture of desire for closeness and fear of vulnerability.

8. When I'm feeling overwhelmed or upset, I prefer my partner to:
   a) Offer support and comfort and help me work through my emotions.
   b) Listen attentively and reassure me of their love and commitment.
   c) Give me space to process my feelings on my own.
   d) Respect my need for space but also check in on me periodically.

9. My past experiences in relationships have been characterized by:
   a) Stability and mutual respect.
   b) Insecurity and a fear of being abandoned.
   c) Independence and a reluctance to depend on others.
   d) Confusion and difficulty navigating emotional connections.

10. When it comes to expressing my needs and desires in a relationship, I tend to:
    a) Feel comfortable communicating openly and directly.
    b) Worry about being perceived as needy or demanding.
    c) Keep my needs to myself to avoid appearing vulnerable.
    d) Struggle to articulate my needs clearly and fear rejection or judgment.

Scoring:

Mostly a's: You likely have a Secure Attachment Style.

Mostly b's: You may have an Anxious-Preoccupied Attachment Style.

Mostly c's: You might have a Dismissive-Avoidant Attachment Style.

Mostly d's: You could have a Fearful-Avoidant (Disorganized) Attachment Style.

Again, consider discussing your responses with a mental health professional for a more thorough evaluation of your attachment style.

Breaking Point

*"Perhaps healing lies **not** in stopping time;*
but in learning to dance with it."

J. DENISE

I was still seeking external validation to fill the void within myself. Yet, as an adult, I realized that validation should stem from within. While I was going through a tumultuous internal struggle, I maintained a facade of strength and composure, perfected over years of practice. But beneath the surface, I was crumbling. Intrusive thoughts were beginning to overwhelm me. It became increasingly difficult to maintain the facade, and I began withdrawing from family and friends, fearing that my secret would be exposed. The negative thoughts and self-blame plagued my mind relentlessly. As my mental state plummeted, intrusive thoughts bombarded me with relentless accusations.

I blamed myself for the trauma I endured, convincing myself that I had somehow invited it, that I hadn't said "no" forcefully enough. Doubts flooded my mind: Who would believe me after all these years? Was I just seeking attention?

What would my parents think? Would they blame themselves for failing to protect me? Would people judge me? Being judged petrified me, especially since I had always been seen as the *strong* one, the pillar of strength for others.

Despite my inner turmoil, I knew I couldn't continue hiding my pain. I needed to confide in someone, but the thought of revealing my traumatic experiences to others, especially when I was the one who always had it "all together," was daunting. To cope, I often resorted to driving alone in my car, with loud music blasting and all the while drowning the thoughts out with alcohol, a temporary escape that only exacerbated my pain. Saunders was the only one who seemed to notice the increase in my indulgence. He addressed my drinking habits, expressing concern that I was indulging too much, which naturally caused me to become defensive.

One day, I found myself unable to drown out the intrusive thoughts. I began to spiral out of control mentally. I attempted to reach out to Saunders, but there was no response. Usually, when the pain became too much to bear, I'd reach out to him, requesting a conversation or a comforting embrace, which he would often accommodate. I desperately needed someone to talk to as the noise in my head grew louder. I refrained from contacting anyone in my immediate family because I didn't want to worry them.

I found myself on the verge of reckless driving behavior on the interstate, driving at dangerous speeds with no regard for my safety or the safety of others. I realized that the faster I drive, the more severe the impact could be. Would this be instant death? Would I finally be free from the pain? These thoughts raced through my mind relentlessly. I screamed out to the Divine for help, and in that moment of pain, the image of my daughter flashed before me, reminding me of the one person who still needed me. Her face served as a wake-up call, jolting me back to reality. How could I consider abandoning her, leaving her to face this world alone? How could I be so selfish? I slowed down, pulled over at the next exit, and collapsed into screams in a nearby parking lot. I just screamed as loud as I could, wanting to cry, but I had no tears. It was a pivotal moment of reckoning, a complete reminder of the precious life depending on me and the responsibility I had as a mother to protect her.

I went into a state of depression, where even my reflection seemed unfamiliar. I describe depression and anxiety as observing a metaphorical clock in my mind. Depression feels as though I'm attempting to stop the clock's hands with one of my hands while simultaneously gathering an assortment of burdens-trauma, heartbreak, bills, etc.-with the other. These burdens weigh you down, yet you find yourself holding onto them, uncertain how to let go. You stare at the accumulation of your hardships, and though mentally it feels as if time stands still, life continues to move forward. This stagnation, this clinging to the past and present burdens, is what I believe triggers depression.

On the other hand, anxiety feels like the complete opposite. It's as if all the burdens you've amassed cause your mental clock's hands to spin uncontrollably fast. You're unable to catch them, overwhelmed by the speed at which time appears to be moving. Despite this rapid passage of time, you continue to accumulate more, fretting over whether there will be enough time to manage everything. However, the focus shouldn't be on the clock at all. Time will move on, regardless of our mental state, so we ought to deal with our burdens in the moment-collecting and releasing them as we proceed through the present. In essence, depression ensues from an attempt to cling to the past, while anxiety stems from an excessive focus on the future rather than living in and dealing with the present moment. It's essential to redirect our thoughts. Ask yourself: What am I experiencing right now?

Amid the darkness consuming me, I masked it well, hiding my struggles from those around me. With a daughter who depended on me, I knew I couldn't stay stagnant. Following the incident, I spent approximately three days lying on the sofa, picturing myself in a casket, a fate I refused to accept. Yet, the simple act of getting up felt challenging, as if I had forgotten how to move. Desperate, I shouted to a higher power for guidance, pleading for strength to break free from this suffocating state. My mental health was deteriorating, and I was increasingly feeling overwhelmed, hopeless, and emotionally distressed.

My therapist explained that I was in a state of mourning because I recognized that my marriage and the life I knew was coming to an end, and I needed to pursue a new direction in my life. She explained that this emotional response is natural and valid, as relationships often hold significant meaning. When a relationship concludes, it can evoke feelings of grief for the loss of companionship, shared experiences, and the future that was once envisioned together. I was mourning not only the relationship itself but also the loss of identity tied to it, as well as the hopes and dreams associated with the partnership.

While I was lying on the sofa, I distinctly heard a voice ask, "Are you going to keep lying here dwindling, or are you going to take control of your life and leave behind what doesn't serve you?" All I felt after that was, I needed to leave. This declaration offered me a path to freedom. But the thought of leaving behind my family, home, and the life I had known for over fifteen years filled me with uncertainty. Doubts crept in as I questioned the implications of such a drastic decision. What about my financial stability? Could I survive on my own? People often sabotage themselves by creating excuses for why they shouldn't act. They may even deny the truth to themselves. At times, I was petrified by the unknown. While I may declare that I deserve better, do I truly understand what "better" entails? People may desire to move forward but fear their past partner will find someone else and treat them better. I've always believed that true readiness is marked by action, not words.

I had contemplated leaving before, but then I discovered I was pregnant with our daughter. The idea of having a broken family was something I couldn't bear, so I chose to stay. Initially, leaving my old life was incredibly difficult because I held my husband in such high regard. I felt compelled to save face for him and avoid the discomfort of explaining our breakup to his family; once again, I found myself prioritizing someone else's feelings over my own. But I knew I needed to find my voice.

Some may perceive me as selfish for prioritizing my emotional needs over my family's. We had been together since we were 17 and 18 years old. Our family, which I often describe as quintessential on paper: high school sweethearts, financially stable, college graduates, and married with a child; wasn't as it appeared. And because others perceived it as such, it made it difficult for me to confide in anyone about my feelings. The relationship was on a pedestal that neither one of us had placed it on. I must make clear that we truly loved each other, but our past experiences made it difficult for us to let down our guard. As a result, our love wasn't expressed as openly as it should have been, however, we shared deep mutual respect and admiration, and we were always willing to support each other in any way we could.

Most people lack understanding of healthy relationships because they learn from their parents' examples. His father was a provider, and my mother was part of a long-term marriage that, in retrospect, lacked emotional depth. My spirit felt unsettled, and the longing for a genuine connection became unbearable despite my fears. I refused to believe this was all I was destined to receive from marriage. I was complacent in that relationship, and I never would have reached my full potential or begun to heal. Everything had fallen into a monotonous routine, and I lacked the motivation to aspire for more. Even with having obtained multiple degrees, I found myself lacking ambition. I ached for a life of fulfillment.

However, as I reflected, I realized that the groundwork for change had already been laid. I had recently secured a new job and built a foundation of financial independence. I also had two crucial questions that demanded honest answers before I could leave; was I prepared to witness him giving someone else everything I had ever requested, and was I ready to potentially spend the rest of my life alone if I didn't find another partner? Once I could genuinely respond "yes" to both questions, that was my confirmation I was prepared to move on. With newfound clarity, I resolved to take control of my destiny. By the time I rose from the sofa, I had made a firm decision to leave behind the shadows of my past and step into a future of empowerment and self-discovery. I needed to do this for myself. I deserved it.

After I left my marriage, I thought I was entering a life of peace; little did I know, this marked the beginning of Divine stripping away all the pent-up pain within me. Now, all my bandages were suddenly stripped away, exposing raw wounds. I feared letting anyone witness my downward spiral, so I withdrew into solitude and isolation. Despite my attempts to patch things up, the bandages refused to hold, and relentless visions plagued me, offering no escape. After years of drowning out these visions in my teenage years, they resurfaced with renewed intensity, leaving me nowhere to hide. The Divine's messages grew louder, impossible to ignore. The more I ran, the deeper I sank into depression. Surrendering became my only option.

With no other choice, I had to confront and heal those wounds. For those struggling to discern the Divine's voice and seeking confirmation of a guided message, understand that it will echo throughout your life. Everywhere you turn, signs and synchronicities will nudge you toward your destined path, offering no respite until you answer your Divine calling. I distinctly recall encounters with strangers urging me to stop running and embrace my purpose. I had to heal. Healing requires a deliberate choice. You must commit your mind to the process, just as you would with any other obstacles in your life. I was displeased with the person I had become after finally exposing my trauma. I wasn't who I thought I was. After years of concealing my pain, I now find myself falling apart, hardly recognizing the person I'm transforming into.

I had no idea what I was feeling when I came across an article that perfectly captured everything I was experiencing at the time. I was experiencing what is often known as the "dark night of the soul," a profound spiritual or existential crisis marked by feelings of emptiness, despair, and inner turmoil. This period is characterized by a deep disconnection from oneself, others, and the Divine. It involves deeply questioning core beliefs, values, and assumptions regarding life, identity, and the nature of existence. It is a time of profound introspection, where individuals confront their deepest fears and doubts. Physical symptoms such as fatigue, insomnia, changes in appetite, or other stress-related health problems may also accompany the emotional and psychological distress of the dark night of the soul. Despite its agonizing nature, the dark night of the soul is often viewed as a transformative journey that ultimately leads to spiritual growth, self-discovery, and a renewed sense of purpose and meaning in life.

CHAPTER FOUR

The Journey of Healing and Personal Growth

Embracing Transformation

Experiencing a traumatic event can often ignite a person's spiritual quest. Dr. Steven Taylor terms this phenomenon "transformation through turmoil" (TTT). He suggests that individuals undergoing this transformation often feel as though they are confronting death and have been utterly shattered. They may find themselves unrecognizable, feeling as if they've hit rock bottom. As a result, a profound transformation of identity takes place, often initiating them into a spiritual journey of awakening and healing. Spiritual awakening and healing are interconnected processes that involve profound shifts in consciousness, self-awareness, and inner transformation.

Spiritual awakening typically refers to a moment or period of realization in which an individual experiences a deep shift in their perception of themselves, others, and the world around them. This awakening often involves a deepening understanding of spiritual truths, a heightened sense of connection to something greater than oneself (such as the divine or universal consciousness), and a sincere sense of inner peace and fulfillment. Spiritual awakening can be activated by a mixture of factors, including intense life experiences, contemplative practices such as meditation or prayer, or encounters with spiritual teachers or teachings.

Healing, on the other hand, involves the process of addressing and resolving emotional, psychological, and spiritual wounds or traumas that have accumulated over time. Healing often requires individuals to confront and work through painful emotions, limiting beliefs, and past traumas to cultivate greater levels of self-love, acceptance, and inner peace. Healing isn't pretty. It's lonely, painful, and full of ups and downs-more a roller coaster than a serene journey. It's not a picturesque scene of art filled with rainbows and sunshine; in reality, it's quite the opposite. You might wonder why people choose to heal. The reason is to reclaim your power, to stop letting the pain and suffering others have inflicted on you control your life. Healing involves confronting and feeling those deep emotions.

Granting yourself grace during the healing process is essential for navigating the complexities of emotional growth and recovery. Be gentle with yourself and acknowledge that healing takes time. It's okay to have moments of vulnerability, feel overwhelmed, or struggle with self-doubt. Recognize that perfection is not attainable. You don't need to have it all figured out or be flawlessly composed at every step. Instead, it's about embracing your imperfections, acknowledging your strengths and limitations, and allowing yourself to learn and grow from each experience.

Don't blame yourself if your feelings for that person or people linger. When you deeply care about someone, those feelings can be persistent; what tends to occur is that you become overly fixated on trying to move on, wondering why you haven't already. This intense focus becomes the primary concern, occupying your thoughts. However, when you continuously dwell on something, you inadvertently reinforce its presence in your mind. Ultimately, giving yourself grace during the healing stage empowers you to cultivate self-compassion and resilience. It allows you to move forward with kindness and acceptance, embracing your journey toward healing with patience, understanding, and love.

Together, spiritual awakening and healing can facilitate extreme personal growth and transformation, leading to greater levels of self-awareness, emotional resilience, and spiritual well-being. They allow you to transcend limiting beliefs and ego-based patterns of thinking and behavior and align more fully with their true essence and purpose in life. Lastly, spiritual awakening and healing are deeply interconnected processes that can lead to greater levels of joy, fulfillment, and spiritual enlightenment. As I embarked on my journey, I recognized the need to rely on God for support.

Although I was raised under Christianity, throughout my life, I often felt judged, and regardless of my efforts, I never seemed to meet the expectations set by religious teachings. Understanding that true healing required me to feel complete in every aspect of my life, I realized I needed to reclaim my relationship with the Divine on my terms. Writing this book became an important moment for me, as I felt a sense of Divine approval and acceptance. In the end, what mattered most to me was knowing that I was pleased with myself, regardless of any potential criticism I might face for diverging from organized religion. Throughout this book, I interchangeably use the labels "God" and "Divine" to refer to the Highest Spiritual Power.

Childhood trauma can bring forth an unfamiliar version of you, leading to a sense of disconnection and confusion about your identity. Sometimes it becomes necessary to seek comfort in something greater than your current state. While I don't associate with the religious teachings of Christianity, I sometimes find wisdom in some of the Bible's symbolic lessons. A scripture from 1 John 4:4

KJV proclaims, "Because greater is he that is in you..." Emphasizing the idea that the presence of God within you is greater, providing guidance, strength, and protection.

Personally, this verse suggests the importance of looking inward to discover the higher aspect of oneself. While some may look outward to the skies or adopt specific physical postures (kneeling), the essence of God, in my understanding, resides within. For me, God represents the ultimate source, the highest expression of oneself, an energy of light and love that surpasses all. Everyone may have their own interpretation and belief system, and it's crucial to lean on those beliefs to navigate life's challenges.

I've come to believe, it's not merely about worshiping but rather the sincerity of your heart and beliefs. I recall a moment when I knelt in prayer, only to hear a Divine message urging me to rise. It dawned on me that remaining in a state of supplication wasn't conducive to reaching my higher self; instead, I needed to take proactive steps toward healing. Despite my initial uncertainty about what "going within" truly entailed, I recognized the necessity of exploring my inner self, even though it meant confronting aspects of myself I had long masked.

I cannot emphasize this enough: when embarking on a spiritual journey or whatever your beliefs are, it's wise to turn to reliable sources, self-help books, and documentaries rather than relying on social media. Many individuals on social media are also navigating their journeys, while others are simply seeking content to share without deep understanding. Relying solely on God and your higher self as your sources of guidance is essential to avoid being misled or confused by the myriad voices on social platforms.

In my own experience, I initially sought answers from external sources instead of trusting my intuition and inner wisdom. It's easy to feel overwhelmed and disoriented by the conflicting information and opinions rampant on social media. Therefore, my advice is to disconnect from social media platforms and enter a period of reflection, embracing solitude, journaling, and communicating with spiritual guides, meditating and praying. By doing so, you can attune yourself to the voice and guidance of the Divine without the distractions and influences of external sources

Everyone has a unique purpose in life, stressing the importance of cultivating a personal relationship with the Divine. While someone else may have admirable ideas and follow a particular path, it doesn't necessarily mean that it's the right path for you. It's essential to align yourself with individuals who resonate with your journey. Continuously joining or recruiting into the wrong group may hinder one's ability to achieve the desired level of success. Sometimes, it's beneficial to navigate your path alone, trusting that those who are meant to accompany you will naturally unite along the journey.

Starting a spiritual and healing journey can be a deeply rewarding and transformative experience. Here are some pieces of advice to consider as you embark on this path:

1. **Set Intentions:** Take some time to reflect on why you want to start this journey. What are your goals? What do you hope to achieve? Setting clear intentions will guide your actions and help you stay focused.

2. **Self-Exploration:** Begin by exploring your beliefs, values, and experiences. Reflect on your past and present and consider how they have shaped you. Journaling, meditation, and introspection can be valuable tools for self-exploration.

3. **Seek Knowledge:** Educate yourself about various spiritual traditions, philosophies, and healing modalities. Read books, listen to podcasts, attend workshops, and

engage with teachers or mentors who resonate with you.

4. **Practice Mindfulness:** Cultivate mindfulness in your daily life by staying,present and aware of your thoughts, feelings, and sensations. Mindfulness practices such as meditation, yoga, and deep breathing can help you develop greater inner peace and clarity.

5. **Connect with Nature:** Spend time in nature to reconnect with the natural world and tap into its healing energy. Whether it's taking a walk in the woods, gardening, or simply sitting outside and observing, nature can be a powerful source of inspiration and rejuvenation.

6. **Listen to Your Inner Voice:** Trust your intuition and inner wisdom as you navigate your journey. Pay attention to the subtle messages and guidance that arise from within and allow them to guide your decisions and actions.

7. **Embrace Healing:** Be open to addressing and healing emotional wounds, traumas, and limiting beliefs that may be holding you back. Seek support from therapists, healers, or support groups if needed, and engage in practices that promote self-care and self-love.

8. **Practice Gratitude:** Cultivate an attitude of gratitude by acknowledging and appreciating the blessings in your life. Regularly expressing gratitude can help shift your perspective and cultivate a positive mindset.

9. **Stay Open-Minded:** Approach your journey with an open mind and a willingness to explore new ideas and perspectives. Be receptive to change and growth and allow yourself to evolve along the way.

10. **Trust the Process:** Remember that healing and spiritual growth are ongoing processes that unfold over time. Be

patient and compassionate with yourself, and trust that you are exactly where you need to be on your journey.

I recognize that everything I endured was necessary for my journey to this point. Each day is a battle to avoid succumbing to darkness, yet embracing every aspect of myself is a must, regardless of the challenges. It wasn't until I embarked on my spiritual path that the purpose behind my struggles became apparent. The lesson that comes from pain often revolves around personal growth, resilience, and self-discovery. Pain can teach you to find strength in adversity, cultivate empathy and compassion, and reassess your priorities and values. It can prompt introspection, leading to a deeper understanding of yourself and others, and ultimately guide you toward a more purposeful and meaningful life. Whether or not there is purpose in pain is deeply subjective; initially confused and questioning why I had to endure so much hurt, I sought to understand the lessons within them rather than allow it to keep me mentally bound.

To know light, you must have gone through darkness. The concept of duality suggests that to appreciate light, one must first experience darkness. This idea contains the notion that contrasting experiences, such as joy and sorrow, pleasure, and pain, are connected and essential for understanding and growth. It's through the contrast of light and darkness that we gain deeper insights into ourselves and the world around us. Darkness can represent challenges, struggles, and moments of gloom, while light symbolizes hope, clarity, and joy. Without experiencing darkness, we may take light for granted or fail to recognize its significance. Similarly, without moments of difficulty, we may not fully appreciate times of ease and happiness.

However, there were times when I felt stagnant in my healing journey, unsure of my next steps and overwhelmed by confusion. In these moments of hopelessness, I turned to God, seeking guidance and clarity. Gradually, I realized that my envisioned life and purpose were far greater than my current circumstances. Yet, I was unsure where to begin. This struggle is common among many of us, we hope for change but are uncertain of how to initiate it. Ultimately, I discovered that the first step is to pause, relinquishing the need to control everything and instead allowing Divine guidance to clarify the path forward.

I believe my purpose was to become a healer for others by tracking my journey and sharing it with them. By reflecting on my own experiences, struggles, and growth, I can offer valuable insights, empathy, and support to those facing similar challenges. Sharing my journey can inspire hope, provide guidance, and foster a sense of connection and understanding among others who may be navigating their paths of healing and self-discovery. Ultimately, my purpose becomes a guiding force in my desire to make a positive difference in the lives of others, using my journey as a source of healing and inspiration.

Finding My Voice

"I made it through the trauma;
I will make it through the healing."

J. DENISE

Though unsure of what this journey would entail, I was determined to pursue it. Recognizing the importance of healing my inner child as a foundational step, I faced challenges due to my lingering trust issues, which made it difficult to speak about my trauma. I reflect on a past moment when I tried to confide in a close relative whom I trusted and believed we shared similar beliefs. I cautiously approached the topic with surface-level conversations, hoping for understanding. However, it became apparent that this person, who has no professional background, began diagnosing me instead of providing the supportive listening ear I needed. While they may have had good intentions, their approach wasn't what I needed at that moment.

This was particularly difficult for me, especially given my fear of judgment. Despite their intentions, I couldn't shake the feeling that their actions didn't stem from a genuine place of understanding or support. Their actions triggered me, exacerbating my trust issues and fear. They silenced me once again. Each time I contemplated revisiting those painful memories, the thought alone intensified my reluctance to share my story. I had allowed countless people to silence me, but it was time to reclaim my voice.

Seeking counseling became an important step for me, and I approached the search with intensity. I did have one specific requirement: I preferred not to work with a black woman from my city. While some may not understand my choice, I knew it was the best decision for my healing journey. I wanted a space where I could be completely open and honest without feeling like I was speaking to one of my relatives. I wasn't ready to disclose my experiences to my family, and the potential familiarity with a counselor/therapist who resembled them would have hindered my willingness to share due to fear of judgment.

Nevertheless, in my quest to find the right fit for my healing journey, I decided to seek therapists with a spiritual background. I selected two counselors and a therapist: one local and the other two non-local. Despite their different locations, they all offered talk-based therapy approaches. In talk therapy, individuals are provided with a safe and confidential space to explore their thoughts, feelings, and behaviors, improve their overall well-being, and address specific concerns or challenges they may be facing.

During talk therapy sessions, individuals may discuss a range of topics, including past experiences, relationships, emotions, and current life circumstances. The therapist or counselor may ask questions, offer insights, and provide guidance to help the individual gain a deeper understanding of themselves and their experiences. I wanted assistance on how to reconnect with those suppressed emotions but found that traditional talk therapy alone wasn't relinquishing the breakthrough I sought.

Unfortunately, the non-local therapist and counselor I engaged with didn't prove to be the right fit for me. One therapist attempted to assign feelings to me that didn't resonate with my own, suggesting medication for depression and anxiety. However, I felt that medicating would merely serve as an escape rather than a true path to healing. Her primary goal was to encourage me to leave my isolation and interact with others, proposing various social events for me to attend. She believed that connecting with new people was essential for my healing process, concerned that my seclusion might hinder it. However, I wasn't prepared to mingle with others yet.

Even before embarking on this journey, I never enjoyed crowded places. I tend to absorb the energies of those around me, which leaves me feeling drained. Deep down, I knew I possessed the strength to confront and overcome my emotions yet fear still held me back. Furthermore, the lack of professionalism displayed by the other counselor, who seemed more captivated by my story, left me disappointed and unsupported in my journey toward healing. It became evident to me that the local therapist was a better match for my needs.

It took me a while to open up to her due to trust issues, fear of judgment, and discomfort with vulnerability. Expressing my feelings was challenging, as I had long suppressed them. It wasn't until about a year into therapy that I finally disclosed the experience of sexual assault. She never pressured me, and she respected my pace. I recall the moment I began to feel more at ease with her. Though seemingly insignificant, after a year of therapy, I noticed that I had shifted from sitting on the sofa's edge to sitting back. This small change marked a significant step forward for me in becoming more comfortable and trusting in therapy.

My therapist suggested an exercise where I would write letters to everyone who had assaulted me and consider sending these letters to them. Although I was uneasy about mailing them, I still wrote the letters. I have included a letter below that I had written to the guy who date-raped me.

To the person who took my power,

When I met you, I thought I met a spiritual man. I was so intrigued that you chose to follow Christ instead of being out in the streets like most guys your age. I had stepped off my walk with Christianity because I found it hard to believe in anything after everything I had gone through in life. However, I started attending church with you and built trust in you. I'd never imagined you would become someone that I would hate. Yes, I know hate is a horrible emotion to feel about anyone, but at 22 years old, I couldn't come up with a better word to describe my feelings. You were no different than the others who violated me.

Despite my clarity about not being ready for a relationship or intimacy, you let jealousy and ego drive your actions. You tricked me to get me alone. You used, manipulated, and hurt me. You only thought of yourself and your needs. You watched the tears roll down my face, and you still proceeded to violate me. I told you I wasn't ready. You seemed to believe I owed you for your time and gifts, though I never sought anything from you. Everything you did for me was because you wanted to do it. I barely knew you. You had no right to make me question my self-worth. You took my free will. For years, I told myself it was my fault because I didn't put up a fight, thinking my lack of resistance was consent. I was frightened and accustomed to surrendering.

My sole focus was returning home to my family. I was aware of the pistol concealed in your black bag. The words you said, "You wanted this. I did this for us," remain etched in my memory. Yet, there was no "us." Your insensitiveness was evident as you observed my expression, knowing I was finished with you. You callously predicted, "You'll be calling me in about a month." How heartless of you. Yet, in my darkest moment, I turned to prayer more earnestly than ever before, pleading. I expressed to God I cannot have my rapist's baby. My prayers were answered, and since then, I haven't seen or heard from you. My therapist suggests forgiveness, but it is myself I forgive first, for you took something irreplaceable. My healing journey began with forgiving myself for the years of power you took from me. I've reclaimed my voice, life, and ability to say no, affirming that the blame was never mine. Now, I stand stronger, with my power restored.

The impact of writing letters to the people who hurt me relieved a heavy emotional burden. It allowed me to express pent-up emotions and confront unresolved feelings, and I gained closure. By putting my thoughts and feelings into words, I was able to externalize my pain and begin the process of letting go. This cleansing brought a sense of release and liberation, allowing me to move forward with greater clarity and emotional freedom. Moreover, it fostered a sense of empowerment, as I reclaimed control over my narrative and asserted my right to heal. Ultimately, writing such a letter was a transformative step towards healing, enabling me to reclaim my inner peace and resilience.

Therapy is an invaluable resource, and while it may not be accessible to everyone due to financial constraints, there are alternative paths to facilitate healing. Therapy served its purpose, yet my struggles with revealing my trauma hindered its effectiveness in fully addressing my healing journey. I recall a moment during meditation when I heard a voice urging me to delve deeper, prompting confusion about what additional steps I needed to take. One day, while reading an article, I stumbled upon the concept of shadow work, a term I had heard before but hadn't fully grasped its meaning.

Shadow work is a psychological concept that involves exploring and integrating the aspects of ourselves that we often repress, deny, or hide; it is the "shadow" aspects of our personality. Spiritual shadow work often incorporates practices such as meditation, mindfulness, journaling, self-inquiry, and introspection to shine a light on unconscious patterns, fears, traumas, and negative beliefs that may be holding us back from reaching our fullest potential. By confronting and accepting these shadow elements with compassion and non-judgment, individuals can transcend limiting beliefs, release emotional blockages, and cultivate inner peace and wholeness. Furthermore, shadow work in spirituality can also involve exploring the collective or ancestral shadow patterns and traumas inherited from our cultural, familial, or societal backgrounds. When you acknowledge and heal these collective wounds, you facilitate your personal growth and contribute to the collective healing and transformation of generations.

As I delved into shadow work and began confronting the wounds I had buried for years, I felt like I was unfolding. It led me to the darkest depths of my being. I distanced myself from friends, family, and even my parents. I withdrew completely, shedding about 30 pounds and sinking into depression. To dismiss concerns about my weight loss, I enrolled in the gym as a diversion. Though the change was noticeable, at least I had a plausible explanation. Isolation left me feeling lost, my once vibrant skin now dull and lifeless. The deeper I went within, the more I felt like I was losing my grip on who I truly was. I questioned how long this torment would endure. Did I even want to heal, or had pain become so ingrained in my identity that I feared letting it go?

Some people won't dare to confront their inner shadows. Exercise caution when evaluating individuals who retreat into their fantasy realm as a coping mechanism for their pain; strive for compassion instead. Shadow work is hard. It was the darkest time of my life. I was isolated, but I still managed to go to work and wear my most essential accessory, my many masks. I was falling apart inside, but I kept up appearances. No one at work suspected anything. Over the years, I went through many changes and created different personas. I just kept adding layers and layers until I lost track of who I was. It's like the saying, a liar can lie so much that they start believing their lies. That's what happens when someone creates a false reality to survive and cope with their trauma.

Numbness enveloped me, and I longed for something, anything, to ease the pain. Then, one Sunday, I sat alone in the center of my bed after a meditation session, I finally cried. I had not cried in years. Tears flowed continuously, my eyes swollen and red, and my body retching. It was a torrent of release, a purging of years of pent-up pain. I knew then that I had to heal; otherwise, I would continue to repeat the same patterns in my life; relationships, whether romantic or platonic. Why was it so challenging for me to embrace self-love and healing? Through this tumultuous journey, I came to understand that my lack of self-love and resistance to healing had kept me trapped in a cycle of stagnation.

At that moment, I decided to free myself from the shackles of my past. I reached out to my middle sister minutes later and revealed everything. Unclear of whether I could trust her to keep my secret or how it might impact her, being aware that she knew of some of the men who had sexually assaulted me. I felt compelled to unburden myself. Silence was no longer an option for me. While she's the only one I confided in, I have no intention of disclosing details to anyone else. That single act of revelation was profoundly liberating for me.

During this period, I began to recognize my deep longing for love, care, support, and, above all, a sense of protection. The only love I knew, without doubt, was the love I have for my daughter flowing effortlessly, like the air I breathe. My maternal grandmother passed away in 2014; I buried the emotions surrounding her death deep within, unable to truly feel the loss. She was an important part of my life, and her absence left a profound void. She was the person I turned to for warmth. It took me nine years after her passing to finally allow myself to grieve, a process that began within my healing journey. I confronted my anger towards her for leaving me feeling abandoned and alone. My grandmother was my everything, my haven, and suddenly she wasn't here anymore. Though it felt selfish, I deeply felt the loss of her presence. Our bond was special and not having her living in this world has been one of my greatest challenges.

I understand love. I have an abundance to offer, yet fear held me back. Numerous unanswered questions flooded my mind. What does it feel like to receive reciprocal love? Why do I feel so undeserving of love? What did I do to deserve this pain? Why did I allow so many people to hurt me? The suffering I experienced was beyond words. My heart felt as though it was shattering, and my body ached with sorrow. I had never cried so profusely or yearned for something so intensely. I questioned what it meant to love myself and whether I had truly tried to do so. I realized that loving myself didn't mean loving others any less; rather, it required me to be whole within myself to love another person genuinely. So why did loving myself feel like such a struggle? I was battling self-doubt and external pressures.

From my unhealed perspective, I wanted to shield others from experiencing the pain I endured. I desired to be a protector and a savior to others, and I felt selfish when prioritizing my needs. Guilt often accompanied moments of self-care, as I felt obligated to help others instead. Furthermore, focusing on myself served as a reminder of my inner turmoil, forcing me to confront past hurt and pain. Making time for self-care became a conscious battle, a constant struggle to prioritize my well-being amidst daily responsibilities. Did I truly know myself? No, I realized I had lived behind a facade for so long that I scarcely knew the authentic me. It was easier to be there for others than to embark on the journey of self-healing. Loving myself felt like a struggle because self-love was hindered by past traumas, societal standards, and accepting my imperfections.

I knew something had to change. I had to rewrite my narrative because I was dissatisfied with the trajectory of my life. I faced a critical decision: remain in a state of unhappiness, allowing the shadows of my past to dominate, or reclaim my strength. I held the pen that shaped this world. I asked myself, will you lie in sorrow and pain, or create an environment where joy and abundance flourish? I started to redefine my narrative to match the life I envisioned for myself.

Acknowledgment is frequently the initial step towards healing. It entails acknowledging and embracing the aspects of us that require attention and nurturing. My inner child craved recognition and validation. I've heard others suggest that to heal your inner child; you should purchase all the items you desired as a child but never received. Yet, what do you buy when all you yearn for is love and protection? I prioritize love over material possessions because, in my upbringing and romantic relationships, gifts lacked emotional significance.

The initial encounter with your inner child can be a profound and transformative experience on your journey of self-discovery and healing. In my initial meeting with my inner child, it occurred in a dream. I found myself seated in a restroom on a chair when a young girl approached me. She spoke with a tone filled with criticism, expressing disappointment as though I had let her down in numerous ways. Her demeanor conveyed profound dissatisfaction. Every time I devoted attention to healing my inner child, progress would halt as I encountered her dissatisfaction, often manifested as anger. It felt as though I was being verbally attacked; negative thoughts flooded my mind, creating an environment of self-bullying. It's a startling realization that one can indeed bully oneself. Consider the inner dialogue during moments of distress or triggers, internalized negativity, harsh criticism, and relentless judgment all constitute forms of self-bullying.

Think about being an adult subjected to bullying by none other than the child within. My efforts never seemed sufficient. Why was I harboring such intense anger toward myself? Why had I neglected and abandoned her for so long? Confronting my inner child became imperative to cease the cycle of self-sabotage. I also remember several occasions when I took my daughter to the park, and she would eagerly ask me to swing with her. However, I found myself unable to leave the car courageously. Witnessing the disappointment in her eyes, I realized it wasn't just a simple reluctance; it was a deeper battle within me. The inner child longed to join her on the swings, yet I felt paralyzed by an overwhelming sadness. It felt like I was denying my inner child the chance to play with others. Despite this, I hesitated to show any vulnerability around my daughter. Discussing it with my therapist, she encouraged me to return to the park as many times as necessary until I found the courage to join her on the swing.

A few days later, I summoned the resolve to step out of the car. As my daughter pleaded for me to push her on the swing, I felt a surge of anxiety overwhelm me. Determined not to disappoint her, I reluctantly approached the swing. With each push, tears welled in my eyes, though I tried to conceal them from her. Feeling embarrassed, I eventually retreated to a nearby bench, watching her with a sense of envy. Watching her enjoy the swings so freely, I couldn't help but feel a bit ashamed as an adult who couldn't muster the courage to join in.

I recognized that to progress, I had to confront my fears head-on and find the courage to get onto the swing. Despite overwhelming anxiety, I gathered the courage to do so, even if only for a moment. The sense of accomplishment and pride that washed over me was gratifying. I had to get my power back. My past had consumed so much of my life. I had to acknowledge what happened to me wasn't my fault, and I am determined not to allow it to hinder me from living my life to the fullest. I understand that I deserve better. Everything I've endured has not been in vain. I needed to prioritize myself.

It became absolute to be mindful of the labels I applied to myself. The words we choose to describe our inner state can significantly impact our reality. Expressions such as "I'm broken," 'I'm hurt," or 'I'm never going to find love again" carry powerful energy that can shape our experiences. When we continually affirm these negative labels, we inadvertently reinforce them within our consciousness, influencing our perceptions and interactions with the world. Our external reality often mirrors our internal beliefs and self- perceptions. Therefore, by consistently labeling ourselves in a negative light, we may attract experiences that validate these beliefs, perpetuating a cycle of pain and limitation.

Why do we struggle to embrace the possibility of better things happening to us? Miracles of life surround us, yet we find it challenging to believe in our worthiness. Many of us are familiar with intrusive thoughts, those persistent whispers of doubt and negativity that seem to hold more weight than positive affirmations. It's as if we're wired to lean towards the negative, perhaps as a means of protecting ourselves from potential disappointment.

Consider this scenario: when faced with reviews of a restaurant or any business, the majority may be overwhelmingly positive, yet the few negative reviews sway our decisions. Despite the abundance of positivity, we fixate on the few instances of criticism, allowing them to overshadow the overall picture. This tendency to prioritize the negative over the positive is deeply ingrained within us, a product of our conditioning and past experiences. But what if we challenge this pattern? What if we consciously focus on the abundance of good around us rather than dwelling on the few instances of negativity? It's a shift in perspective that requires effort and intentionality but can lead to profound changes in how we perceive ourselves and the world around us. So, the next time doubt creeps in and threatens to overshadow your belief in better things, remember this: you are worthy of joy and of all the good that life has to offer. It's simply a matter of choosing to believe in the possibility of greater things, even in the face of uncertainty.

To manifest the life you desire, you must actively materialize it. Materialization in healing refers to the process of manifesting physical or tangible changes or improvements because of inner healing work. It involves transforming emotional, mental, or spiritual healing into tangible outcomes or manifestations, such as improved relationships, better health, or increased abundance. Steps to materialization involve several key processes:

Visualize: This entails creating a clear mental image or vision of what you desire to manifest in your life. Visualizing allows you to focus your intentions and energies toward a specific goal or outcome. Visualize the most healed and healthy version of you. Envision yourself engaging in activities you enjoy, feeling energized and vibrant. I love being around water, so I always visualize myself on a tropical island with beautiful blue water and palm trees.

Verbalize: Verbalizing involves expressing your desires and intentions through words or affirmations. By speaking positively about your goals and aspirations, you reinforce your belief in their attainment and align your thoughts with your desired reality. Speaking positively about your healing journey can reinforce belief in your ability to overcome challenges and promote a sense of empowerment.

Emotionalize: Emotionalizing refers to infusing your visualizations and affirmations with strong positive emotions. By feeling deeply connected to your desires and experiencing the joy, gratitude, and excitement associated with achieving them, you amplify the power of your intentions and attract them into your life more effectively. Emotions play a powerful role in shaping our experiences and influencing outcomes. In healing, cultivating positive emotions can reduce stress and enhance overall well-being.

Actualize: Actualizing involves taking concrete steps towards your goals; by translating your visions and affirmations into tangible actions and behaviors, you actively contribute to bringing your desires to fruition and manifesting the life you envision. In healing, actualizing involves implementing healthy behaviors, moving towards wholeness or completeness, and making lifestyle changes that support your well-being.

When I began my healing process, I noticed that anytime I started feeling overwhelmed, I'd rationalize my thoughts and talk myself through them. I read somewhere that this was just another way to suppress emotions. For me, being vulnerable was incredibly difficult; it made me feel weak, and embracing my femininity was particularly challenging. I had to learn to sit with my emotions, whether I experienced hurt or disappointment, and stay with them; it's only by fully experiencing these feelings that you begin to process them and understand how your body reacts. Once you achieve this understanding, you can finally let go.

When intrusive thoughts or images arise, I now catch them and remind myself to "change," shifting my focus to something positive. These thoughts often stem from trauma, stress, depression, or anxiety and can unexpectedly surface at any time. It's important not to dwell in negativity; instead, I stay present and in control of my thoughts. I've repeated "change" so frequently that it echoes in my dreams. Being mindful of my thoughts, I incorporate daily affirmations to shape the reality I seek. We must not only be aware of our thoughts but also of the words we speak. Proverbs 18:21, for instance, highlights the profound impact of our words on our lives: "Death and life are in the power of the tongue." It symbolizes the profound influence of our words on shaping our reality and the importance of speaking positively to manifest a life of abundance and purpose. While these negative thoughts may feel overwhelming, they don't manifest unless we consciously intend them to. Our minds operate in conscious and subconscious states, influencing our perceptions and experiences.

I consciously reframe negative self-talk and replace opposing labels with affirmations that reflect empowerment, resilience, and self-love. By affirming statements such as "I am healing," "I am capable of love," or "I am deserving of happiness," I shifted my internal dialogue towards positivity and possibility. Through mindful self-labeling, I cultivate a more supportive and nurturing relationship with myself. I recognize that my words hold creative power and that I can shape my reality through intentional language and thought. By affirming my innate worthiness and potential, I opened myself to infinite possibilities and experiences grounded in love, healing, and abundance.

Don't regret the choices you've made in your life. You were merely responding to what you believed you needed at the time, and sometimes, our thoughts and emotions can lead us astray. It's through growth and healing that we come to understand this. I recall coming across an old post on social media where I mentioned feeling spoiled and easily hurt when things didn't go my way. In retrospect, I realized it wasn't about being spoiled; rather, I longed for reciprocity. I wanted someone to support me as I supported them. I used my birthday to demand this attention, making it known from the first day of April until the last day. Though it may have annoyed others, they went along with my plans, whether they wanted to or not. My birthday was the one occasion I felt assured that people would acknowledge me.

Some people discover what draws others to them and capitalize on it; whether it's a positive or negative trait. This can become a dependency, happening consciously or unconsciously. For example, someone naturally empathetic may find that people are drawn to them for emotional support, and they may consciously cultivate and utilize this trait to deepen their relationships. On the other hand, someone may unintentionally rely on negative behaviors, such as manipulation or deceit, to gain attention or control in relationships. In both cases, individuals may recognize what attracts others to them and use it to their advantage, whether for better or worse. Also, someone who struggles to maintain employment may find themselves consistently receiving financial support from others; rather than striving for improvement, they cling to this dynamic.

There reaches a point where you desire only genuine individuals in your circle, and you must cease attempting to compel people to be present in your life. Some individuals chase a thrill rather than forming authentic connections with others. Often, those we desire affection or attention from may not genuinely care about us. If you have to coerce someone to be there for you, they're probably not the type of person you want in your life, be it in friendships, family, or romance. It's essential to learn to rely on yourself to find validation. We can create the family we need; family isn't always biological. Surround yourself with people who genuinely love and support you unconditionally. Until you find your tribe/family, take solace in loving yourself.

I give myself daily affirmations, even with tears in my eyes. I strive to become the best version of myself, even when the journey feels difficult. I won't sugarcoat it; this journey is challenging. It was one of the most challenging decisions I have made, but it was undeniably worth it. There were mornings when I'd dance in front of the mirror, calling myself beautiful and reciting self-affirmations. Then there were mornings when I couldn't muster the energy to leave my bed, overwhelmed by self-doubt and sadness. I'd go from praising to questioning my circumstances in the blink of an eye.

Some days, I wanted to hide away and give up hope. I had to allow myself to experience these emotions without judgment or suppression. I was feeling detached, spending weeks in solitude, but learning to be gentle with myself. Also, there were days when I felt weak and physically ill, but I knew I had to persevere; there was no turning back. Once I removed the mask, I knew I could never put it back on; my soul wouldn't allow it. I had to tell myself not to let anyone dictate or rush my journey. Remember, this journey is all about self. "Self" is the keyword here. I've discovered my voice and refuse to be silenced or used again. Saying "no" has become a strength and a norm.

Setting Boundaries

Many individuals carry hidden trauma, and it's impossible to predict which version of them you might encounter. Learning and establishing healthy boundaries is a wise approach when first meeting them. Without clear examples of healthy boundaries, trauma victims may struggle to identify and communicate their own needs and limits in relationships. Unhealthy boundaries can manifest in various ways, such as over-sharing, revealing too much personal information to others, even when it's not necessary or appropriate, and getting involved in intimate connections with people you barely know or have just met. They adopt people-pleasing behaviors as a coping mechanism, prioritizing the needs of others over their own to avoid conflict or gain approval.

Even though I was very private, following a prolonged period of silence, I found myself sharing excessively with anyone who would lend an ear. All I truly wanted was someone who would listen, only to have my concerns minimized by those who believed their struggles were greater. This newfound openness triggered deep- seated wounds of abandonment within me. It became apparent that others were accustomed to my consistent support without me requiring reciprocity. Feeling vulnerable, I noticed a sense of dependency within myself. I realized people were not interested in hearing about my battles. They assumed I had a good life and dismissed my need for support as attention-seeking behavior. I never tried to portray myself or my relationship as perfect; I chose not to share details, not out of a desire to conceal anything, but because people seemed indifferent. I've come to understand that others often view your relationship through the lens of their deficiencies. Since I was not a single mother and had financial support, it seemed I wouldn't have any significant problems. On occasions when people did listen, their reactions were either met with silence or a sudden need to end the conversation. My phone rang only when others sought a need for me to show up for them, yet when it was my turn to share, their disinterest was unmistakable. Consequently, I stopped sharing.

If you tend to give a lot, it's important to acknowledge that takers are often quick to recognize this dynamic. No matter how much you give, it may never be sufficient for some individuals. You could exhibit unlimited kindness, consistently showing up for them in every aspect, yet they may never acknowledge your efforts. Some people are unwilling to recognize your value, compassion, and thoughtfulness; even if you're the sole source of love and support they have ever encountered, they might refuse to acknowledge it and persist in manipulating you. Understanding certain individuals is dedicated to exploiting others, and no matter how much effort you put in reciprocity and appreciation may always remain elusive. It's crucial to recognize your worth and detach yourself from these individuals. When you consistently let manipulative and abusive people into your life, you're only harming yourself. Those who have experienced brokenness often seek to heal others to shield them from similar pain.

Most individuals who have experienced childhood trauma tend to follow a path toward either empathy or self-contentedness. For those who have become empaths as a result of their trauma, helping others can be both rewarding and daunting. It's like reliving your past hardships, which can feel overwhelming. Assisting someone gives you a sense of accomplishment and purpose, making you feel needed and responsible for their wellbeing. Conversely, interacting with someone who is mentally stable might make you feel like you're not needed, as they don't seem to require your help. Thus, empaths often seek new "projects" rather than addressing their issues, seeking a sense of belonging through these endeavors. Trying to change someone into something they're not ready or able to be is counterproductive; you should love them from a distance. Ironically, this drive to help others can also be a way of avoiding your unresolved trauma.

However, as I progressed in my healing, I became aware of how I was inserting myself into the affairs of others and interfering in their lives. It became evident that people reached out to me solely when they needed my assistance, energy, and nurturing. I needed to learn to refrain from excessively involving myself in the lives of others. While they may welcome my help when it suits them, it was perceived as overbearing when they didn't want it. Inadvertently, it all stemmed from an authentic place. I now understand that showing genuine love isn't about always making myself available for others. It's about allowing individuals the freedom to be themselves, even if it means letting go.

True love is unconditional acceptance and support without ego-driven agendas. It's also about honoring their journey and empowering them to pursue their desires independently. Some people see unconditional love as accepting anything, measuring it by their ability to withstand it. While offering support when needed, it's important to establish boundaries. Sometimes, it means stepping back to allow them to pursue their desired life relationships or address personal struggles on their terms. Continuously enduring pain inflicted by someone you love is not ideal. Unconditional love can sometimes turn into unconditional tolerance. I had to allow people the space to grow and evolve on their terms without relying on me as their crutch or guide. Not everyone was receptive to my assistance; they've grown comfortable with their brokenness and have resigned themselves to defeat. I asked myself, "Who are you to challenge their perspective?" The only person I'm responsible for is myself. Rather than attempting to fix someone else, I needed to focus on my personal growth. I had to understand why I tolerated mistreatment and why I believe it's acceptable to give everything to others without leaving anything for myself. Often, we're as broken as the people we're trying to mend.

Meanwhile, my own life was in disarray and lacked direction and passion. Yet, I found myself drafting business plans, creating resumes and so much more for others. It became clear that I needed to prioritize my journey and refrain from attempting to rescue others before rescuing myself. I began to invest in my growth. These individuals I supported never returned the support. After all, reciprocity was never expected in the past. If they could rely on me without reciprocating the same energy, why should they feel obligated to reciprocate now? Some deliberately weren't interested in my achievements or well-being and only sought to exploit me, while others, not out of unwillingness, simply could not offer support. Instead of criticizing them, I learned to establish boundaries to safeguard my well-being.

When Divine guides you into isolation, you start losing relationships you might not have otherwise left behind. I recall praying for the removal of anyone who wasn't aligned with my path, unaware of the close bonds I would lose. Initially puzzled by the departures, I sought clarity. The revelations were painful. Losing individuals who had been part of my life for years wasn't easy to accept, yet, seclusion, while challenging, brought a sense of peace that made it worthwhile.

People can drain your energy, and I had to reclaim my power and energy from those who were using it without my consent. You discover the art of loving them from a distance, and if someone must remain in your life, ensure that you establish clear boundaries. I accepted that some people serve as mere distractions on my journey. Instead of attempting to change them, I focused on adjusting how I engage with them.

Choosing to walk away from emotionally unavailable individuals and those who no longer served me, whether it was my parents, friends, family, or romantic partners, was an act of self- preservation and self-respect. It involved identifying my worth and prioritizing my emotional health and happiness. By disengaging from relationships or situations that drained my energy or hindered my personal growth, I created spaces for healthier connections and experiences.

Although difficult, walking away allowed me to honor my needs and boundaries, paving the way for greater fulfillment and authenticity in my life. This journey of self-discovery and healing taught me the importance of looking inwardly for the love and approval I craved. It became clear that true contentment and wholeness could only come from within, not from someone else's actions or affections. The ability to let go of what no longer served me was not an act of abandonment but profound self-care, setting the stage for a life where I could thrive, not just survive.

Exiting a long-term marriage or relationship is undeniably challenging, especially with children involved. However, children must witness both parents leading fulfilled lives. When you prioritize your needs, it's best to proceed quietly. When I decided to leave, I kept it to myself; nobody was aware of my next step until it was secured. While family may mean well, they can inadvertently hinder your progress. If they fail to understand your path, you may encounter them projecting their fear or disapproval onto you. This fear may prevent you from taking risks, pursuing your passions, or exploring new opportunities that could foster growth and self- realization. When I moved, I received no assistance whatsoever. I handled the entire move alone. While I didn't expect family support, I was not discouraged, as their loyalty and love for Jay was understandable given his longstanding presence in their lives and made him truly part of the family. The absence of support during my move deepens my appreciation for the experience.

While I developed a newfound appreciation for myself, the lack of support still came with its own set of triggers; even though I physically moved, mentally, I was stuck. Nowhere felt like home. In my apartment, I bought only the essentials-sofa, beds, TVs-not because I couldn't afford more, but because the thought of fully decorating was daunting. My previous house was well decorated, but this apartment remained stark, without a single picture on the walls and no other accessories. My family urged me to personalize it, unaware of the mental anguish the idea of adding more "things" caused me. I constantly worried about who would help me move if I needed to relocate.

The more possessions I acquire, the more items I'll need to pack up and move on my own if I change locations. Many didn't know that I never hung up my clothes; instead, I kept them in bags and totes, always prepared for a potential move. I couldn't shake off the feeling of unease, and I wasn't sure why. It wasn't about regretting my decision; rather, it was difficult for me to release myself mentally from the situation of not having support. The thought of it saddened me deeply because I had always been there for others. Despite some initial promises of help, when the time came, no one showed up. Yet, I wasn't resentful; I understood that this was a task I had to tackle on my own. I harbored no expectations; no one was obligated to assist me.

Staying mentally stuck, even after making physical changes, is a complex phenomenon that can deeply affect someone's overall well-being. This often happens because our external actions, like moving to a new place, are not always synchronized with our internal emotional states. When significant issues from the past are not fully processed or resolved, they can create a mental block that prevents you from fully engaging with and embracing new circumstances. This might mean feeling detached or disinterested in a new home or unable to form new relationships despite physical relocation. The mind often develops protective strategies that can become barriers to moving on. These mechanisms, such as emotional numbing or avoidance, might have been useful in the past but can become hindrances, preventing full emotional engagement with the present.

Pain, disappointment, and hurt are unavoidable aspects of life; it's important to acknowledge that they will arise at times and be prepared to handle them effectively. Knowing when to detach from the source of disappointment, pain, or hurt can be crucial for preserving my emotional health. This didn't mean I continued suppressing or avoiding my feelings, but rather recognizing when a situation was causing me undue harm and taking steps to protect myself. By setting healthy boundaries and practicing self-care, I navigated painful experiences with greater resilience and grace. At times, it was necessary to distance myself from certain situations to gain clarity and perspective. We often become so absorbed in what people tell us that we overlook what their actions reveal. It's easy to cling to what's familiar, even when it's not treating us well, whether with family, friends, or romantic relationships. Sometimes, fear holds us back from leaping. However, if your current situation is draining and not healthy, you must trust that whatever comes next will be much better.

Moving away allowed me to observe the situation from an objective standpoint, free from the immediate emotions and pressures that may cloud my judgment. This separation provided valuable insight, enabling me to assess the situation more accurately and make informed decisions about how to proceed. Consider, for example, this scenario I crafted involving the character, Tara.

Tara grew up in a large family with a very authoritarian culture where conformity was emphasized over individual expression. Criticism from her family members was common and often harsh, and Tara always felt pressured to live up to her family's strict standards and expectations. Over the years, Tara began to recognize how much this environment stifled her dreams and personality. She had a passion for art and travel, which her family often dismissed as impractical and frivolous.

As Tara entered adulthood, the stress and anxiety of constantly trying to please her family began to take a toll on her mental and emotional health. Encouraged by a supportive friend, Tara began to explore her interests more deeply, enrolling in art classes and saving money for small trips. Each step she took toward pursuing her interests built her confidence and sense of self-worth. However, whenever she shared these new experiences with her family, she was met with skepticism or outright disapproval.

Feeling increasingly alienated and misunderstood, Tara made the difficult decision to distance herself from her family's negativity. She communicated to them that while she valued her roots, she needed space to grow into the person she was discovering herself to be. Tara began to limit her time at family gatherings and shared less about her personal life during conversations. This decision brought mixed emotions for Tara. She felt liberated and more aligned with her true self, yet also dealt with feelings of isolation and guilt for distancing herself from her family. Over time, Tara built a life-filled with activities and people who supported and appreciated her passions, she found a new sense of belonging and happiness.

Tara's story highlights the importance of setting boundaries for personal growth, especially when familial expectations are suffocating. By choosing to prioritize her well-being and interests, Tara not only preserved her mental health but also started building a fulfilling life that was authentically hers. While this story is fictional, I find resonance in it because, like the character, I, too, embarked on a journey to find fulfillment in life. I began to strive for fulfillment rather than solely pursuing happiness. While happiness is often fluctuating and dependent on external factors, fulfillment is more enduring and rooted in a sense of purpose, meaning, and contentment. Fulfillment transcends momentary moods and temporary pleasures, providing a deeper and more sustainable source of life satisfaction. By focusing on activities, relationships, and goals that align with my values and bring meaning to my life, I can cultivate a sense of fulfillment that sustains me through both joyful and challenging times.

As I progress on my journey, it's important to prioritize ongoing healing and acknowledgment of my inner child. This entails recognizing and tending to the emotional wounds and needs that originated in childhood. By regularly engaging in practices that nurture and validate my inner child, such as self-compassion, self- care, and inner reflection, I can foster deeper healing and wholeness within myself--remembering to approach this process with patience, gentleness, and empathy, allowing me the time and space needed to honor and integrate all aspects of my inner self.

Questions might arise about whether Jay and I considered couples counseling. We discussed it, but reaching a mutual agreement proved challenging. Ultimately, I chose a different path for my life, recognizing the importance of healing on my terms. It's essential to understand that not everyone is ready to embark on such a journey simultaneously; every person must do what they feel is right for themselves. I hope that if he ever feels the need to seek counsel, he will take that step. Naturally, he will have my full support. As for me, I was ready, and consequently, I pursued therapy and healing separately from our union. It's important to cultivate a sense of personal agency and empowerment in our healing process while also acknowledging and appreciating the support that others can provide along the way. While others can offer support, guidance, and love, expecting them to single-handedly fix us may place undue pressure on them and set unrealistic expectations.

For years, I relied on Jay to fill the void within me. I hoped his love, validation, and presence would be enough to mend the broken pieces. As I stepped away from the confines of our marriage, I saw with a clarity that was both liberating and sobering: no matter what Jay did, it wouldn't have been enough to satisfy me. Similarly, I sought unwavering love from my parents, longing for their validation and recognition. I yearned to be acknowledged and treated equally to my siblings, hoping to experience the same warmth I believed they received. However, I began to understand that people can only offer what they can give.

In the solitude of my newfound freedom, I was forced to confront the harsh reality that I lacked self-love. I had spent so long seeking external validation, grasping at fleeting moments of affirmation from others to patch up the deep wounds within me. But the truth was, no one else could heal me; no amount of love, no words of encouragement, and no grand gestures could fill the void that lived within. I realized that my husband, my parents, my friends, or anyone else for that matter, could fix me. They could offer support, and they could lend a listening ear, but ultimately, the journey of healing was mine and mine alone to assume. I found the power to fix myself.

Discovering the love, I craved within myself has led to new insights into external relationships; in my family, this shift has brought about a newfound sense of acceptance and understanding. By embracing my imperfections and vulnerabilities, I've learned to extend the same compassion and empathy to my family members, fostering deeper connections built on mutual respect and unconditional love. Rather than seeking validation or approval from my family, I've learned to appreciate them for who they are, flaws and all, and to cherish the unique bond we share.

Similarly, in my friendships, discovering self-love has transformed how I interact with them; I've become more attuned to my own needs and boundaries, allowing me to cultivate friendships based on mutual respect, trust, and reciprocity. Instead of seeking validation or approval from my friends, I've learned to value myself for who I am and to surround myself with people who uplift and support me unconditionally. This shift has allowed me to adapt deeper, more meaningful connections with friends who share my values and aspirations, enriching my life in ways I never thought possible.

In past romantic relationships, I often emphasized that my partner was "wanted, not needed." This mindset prevented me from fully investing in the relationship and/or settling for the bare minimum. If something wasn't reciprocated or done, I had the belief that I didn't need their assistance anyway. My perspective has since shifted to viewing my partner as needed. I've realized that I can maintain my independence while also relying on my significant other to be there for me and reciprocate the same level of energy I offer. I will not expect anything from my partner that I am not willing or ready to offer. This can enhance both our sense of desirability and importance in the relationship. My needs for him are:

When I'm unable to support myself emotionally, I need him to step in and pour into me as I would do for him. I need him to take responsibility for his actions. I need him to support me when life becomes overwhelming, or others oppose me. I need him to take on a leadership role. I need him to possess spiritual awareness. I need him to prioritize romance as much as he does the sexual aspect of our relationship. I need him to have confidence in his role as my significant other and, most importantly, in himself. I need him to be complete within himself and understand that being vulnerable and emotionally present is acceptable. I need him to regard me as his confidante and support system rather than an adversary. I need him to be mindful of his capabilities. I need him to recognize the significance of prioritizing self-care for both of us. I need him to understand that if we aren't separately complete, our union can't be whole. He needs to acknowledge that we're in a partnership and be at ease seeking comfort from me when he falls short, mentally or financially. Overall, I need his emotional, physical, financial, and spiritual support and presence.

I appreciate all the relationships and friendships I've experienced that contributed to my growth. They've brought light to areas in my life that needed healing; at times, I may have been too demanding for some and not present enough for others. I now realize it was selfish to expect others to fix parts of myself that I wasn't willing to address. Knowingly, although I may have endured something traumatic, it doesn't define who I am.

I am now fortunate to have a tight-knit circle of family and friends who show care and support for me. Despite the lack of reciprocity, which I've often encountered in the past, I am committed to remaining true to myself and always ready to help, but now with clear boundaries in place. No one holds dominion over me, and my journey toward healing showcases my path to distinctly demonstrate my evolution and determination to improve in all relationships. I am committed to continuously striving to be a supportive presence to friends and family members, but all this comes with limits. I embrace that it's acceptable to put myself first. It's okay to end any relationship that no longer benefits me, regardless of its nature or duration. Even as I prioritize myself, I can still be kind.

I understand that continuing growth and healing processes are vital for my personal development, contribute to healthier relationships with myself and others, and foster a sense of purpose and meaning in life. However, setting boundaries may not always be met with understanding or acceptance from others. Some individuals may push back or attempt to violate your constraints, which can be challenging. In these situations, stand firm within your boundaries and prioritize your well-being. As I continue my healing journey, I remember it requires practice, patience, and self-compassion.

Practicing self-compassion is a beautiful gift you can give yourself; it involves treating yourself with kindness, understanding, and acceptance, especially during challenging times. I must be gentle with myself as I learn to navigate this new territory and know how to adjust as needed. Ultimately, I must embrace this journey with courage and confidence, knowing I deserve love, respect, and happiness. My journey has been filled with challenges and obstacles, but I aspire for it to be a source of inspiration and learning for others.

Practices for Growth and Renewal

*"As soon as healing takes place,
go out and heal somebody else."*

MAYA ANGELOU

Approaching healing and personal growth encompasses purposeful methods focused on overcoming obstacles, nurturing resilience, and improving overall wellness. In the process of healing, maintaining a positive mindset is key. I started prioritizing the content I consumed, paying close attention to the music, podcasts, and social media I engaged with. It was imperative to surround myself with content that aligns with the mindset I aim to cultivate.

In addition to the content I consumed, I became mindful of the people I chose to surround myself with. I knew I had to select people who uplifted and supported my healing journey. Healing is not a destination but rather an ongoing journey, marked by moments of progress and setbacks. Along this journey, individuals may encounter triggers-events, situations, or memories that evoke strong emotional reactions or memories associated with past trauma or pain. These triggers have the potential to disrupt the healing process and bring forth feelings of distress, anxiety, or sadness.

However, they also present opportunities for growth and self-awareness. How you respond to these triggers doesn't necessarily reflect your progress. It's easy to pretend to be healed in isolation. It's simple to intellectualize your avoidance as protecting peace when nothing challenges you or disturbs your composure. The real test of healing comes when you're reintegrated into the same environment and no longer experience the same outcomes or feel the same level of fear, dread, or anxiety. It is important to me that I give myself grace when I am triggered. I take a moment to pause and focus on my breath, acknowledge and validate my emotions without judgment. I remind myself that it's okay to feel what I'm feeling and that my feelings are valid. After the trigger has passed, I take the time to reflect on what triggered me and explore any underlying emotions or beliefs that arise.

This process enables me to identify my triggers and gain better control over them. Below are the practices I used to help me on my healing journey. Healing is not a one-month endeavor; it requires consistent dedication over time. Engaging in healing practices should become a lifestyle rather than a temporary fix.

Shadow work. Shadow work forces you to go deep inside and peel off all those layers you've created until you can't see any light; everything is so dark. This involves confronting and embracing all your hidden fears, traumas, insecurities, and other aspects of self that have been repressed or denied. Through shadow work, I gain profound insights into my subconscious patterns and behaviors, leading to greater self-awareness, healing, and personal growth.

It's humbling to realize how little you truly know yourself. I found myself wondering, how did I build so many walls around me that I had to ask who I was? I had to be vulnerable, and I felt exposed, thinking people could see through the façade; that I was not who I claimed to be. I didn't have it all together. And here I was, advising people about being their true selves and showing up for them when I had no idea who I was. I hid behind all those college degrees because that's where I felt the most liberated.

Concurrently, I kept myself from speaking about my accomplishments because fear held me back from reaching my full potential and caused a sense of embarrassment. I also wished to avoid appearing boastful. Feeling needed and being there for others gave me purpose and belonging, even though I never truly felt like I fit in anywhere. Ironically, I could adjust to any situation I was in; nothing ever felt like home. Every setting felt unnatural. Through engaging in shadow work, I dismantled barriers, uncovered the underlying reasons for suppressing many of my emotions, and understood why I reacted in specific situations.

Journaling. This practice became my primary focus, helping me articulate thoughts on paper and clear my mind. Video journaling became essential during my travels, offering a dynamic method to capture emotions and tones. Journaling throughout my healing process provided a haven for introspection and expression. It allowed me to process emotions effectively, gain clarity on my thoughts, and track my progress. Journaling proved therapeutic, enabling the exploration of experiences, identification of patterns, and insights into my healing journey.

Additionally, journaling fosters self-awareness and mindfulness, enabling me to cultivate an understanding of myself and my needs. When I began journaling, I found myself flooded with many questions, but lacking answers.

Why did this occur? Why did I fall short? Why doesn't anyone love me? And so on. Over time, you'll find yourself capable of filling in the gaps and addressing many of your questions. Journaling can take on an informal tone. It's important to avoid self-judgment while writing and to extend yourself some compassion. You have the freedom to be as candid and open as necessary. Whether you keep or discard your notes is entirely up to you. However, keeping your journal allows you to revisit past entries, reflect on your progress, and see how your thoughts and feelings have evolved.

Self-Care. Another essential part of healing is self-care. Self-care allows you to prioritize yourself, ensuring that you replenish your physical, emotional, and mental reserves and spiritual growth so that you can show up fully in your life and for others. Remember, self-care is not selfish; it's an essential foundation for living a balanced and gratifying life. Prioritizing self-care allows us to manage stress, prevent burnout, and cultivate resilience in life's challenges. It enables us to show up as our best selves in relationships, work, and daily activities. Here are some essential practices:

1. **Prioritize Physical Health:** Ensure you're getting adequate rest, nutrition, and exercise. Physical well-being provides a solid foundation for emotional resilience. This proved to be the most challenging aspect of self-care. With my mind and schedule being constantly active, I had to discover how to switch off at times and prioritize time to recharge.
2. **Embrace Emotional Expression:** Allow yourself to feel and process emotions without judgment. Practice journaling, meditation, or talking to a trusted friend or therapist.
3. **Set Boundaries:** Establish healthy boundaries to protect your energy and limit interactions that drain you emotionally or mentally.

4. **Engage in Activities You Enjoy:** Dedicate time to hobbies, interests, or activities that bring you joy and relaxation. This helps to counterbalance the challenges of healing.

5. **Practice Self-Compassion:** Treat yourself with kindness and understanding, acknowledging that healing is a journey with ups and downs. Offer yourself the same compassion you would extend to a loved one.

6. **Seek Support:** Surround yourself with a supportive network of friends, family, or a therapist who can offer encouragement, validation, and guidance.

7. **Mindfulness and Meditation:** Incorporate mindfulness practices or meditation into your daily routine to cultivate present-moment awareness and reduce stress.

8. **Limit Exposure to Triggers:** Identify and minimize exposure to triggers that exacerbate emotional distress or trauma reactions.

9. **Celebrate Progress:** Acknowledge and celebrate small victories and milestones along your healing journey, no matter how minor they may seem.

10. **Practice Patience:** Healing is a gradual process, so be patient with yourself and allow yourself the time and space needed to heal at your own pace.

11. **Listen to Positive Music-** Address physical, emotional, cognitive, and social needs. It involves the use of musical elements such as rhythm, melody, harmony, and lyrics to facilitate non-verbal communication, expression of emotions, and relaxation.

Spiritual Grounding. Grounding involves harmonizing the spiritual and physical energies within oneself by establishing a connection with the Earth. Despite not being naturally inclined towards outdoor activities, I discovered the healing power of spending time in natural settings, whether it was a park or a serene body of water, being outdoors became a cherished pastime for me. There's always been a deep affinity within me for water, whether it's the soothing rhythm of waves at the beach or the tranquil stillness of a lake or pond. Surprisingly, I found myself drawn to kicking off my shoes and sinking my feet into the grass, basking in the warmth of the sun; this newfound appreciation marked a significant shift from my previous aversion to being barefoot outdoors. Through the connection with nature, I experienced a profound sense of peace and rejuvenation; this transformation allowed me to embrace the harmony of the natural world and become attuned to its rhythms.

Reparenting. I am committed to maintaining boundaries and have embraced reparenting myself, which enables me to foster a harmonious connection with my inner child. Reparenting allows me to give myself the love and affection I did not receive as a child. It has taught me how to unlearn all the unhealthy cycles passed down through generations. I now take on the role of my parents. I can heal childhood wounds that have developed because of my needs not being met through inner child healing, meditation, and shadow work. Reparenting is normally facilitated under the supervision of a licensed therapist, but I decided to do it independently. Realizing the significant influence journaling had on my healing journey, I wanted to share the prompts I used, so I developed a guided journal aimed at helping inner child reparenting. "Reparenting Your Inner Child: A Self Help Guided Journal for Women" and "Reparenting Your Inner Child: A Self Help Guided Journal for Men." You can find these journals on Amazon.

Therapy. Seeking therapy provided me with a non-judgmental space where I could freely express my concerns. Despite my initial hesitation, my therapist skillfully guided me to open up and share my thoughts and feelings. Therapists are trained professionals who can provide support, guidance, and practical tools to help individuals navigate through challenging situations, cope with stressors, and work toward personal growth and healing. Therapy offers an opportunity for individuals to gain insight into themselves, develop healthier coping mechanisms, and learn effective strategies for managing emotions and relationships. Addressing underlying issues and building resilience, therapy can empower individuals to lead more fulfilling and balanced lives.

In summary, my use of these comprehensive approaches to healing encompassed engaging in shadow work to explore suppressed aspects of myself, journaling for self-reflection, practicing self-care for physical and emotional well-being, reparenting to address unmet childhood needs, spiritual grounding for inner peace, therapy for professional support, and growth. These practices collectively promote emotional healing, self-awareness, and personal development.

The journey from unhealed to healing is often a profound and transformative process, marked by significant personal growth and introspection. Initially, the person may find themselves grappling with unresolved trauma, emotional scars, and deep-seated wounds from past experiences, such as childhood trauma or abusive relationships. These unresolved issues can manifest in various ways, including difficulty forming healthy relationships, struggles with self- esteem, and patterns of self-destructive behavior.

However, the journey of healing begins with a willingness to confront these inner demons and confront the pain head-on. This may involve seeking therapy or counseling to work through past traumas, engaging in self-care practices such as mindfulness or meditation, and cultivating a supportive network of friends and loved ones who can offer guidance and encouragement.

As a person progresses along their healing journey, they may experience moments of insight and self-discovery. They may learn to set healthy boundaries, practice self-compassion, and release themselves from the shackles of their past. Through this process, they reclaim their power and agency, recognizing that they can shape their destiny and create a life filled with meaning and purpose.

Ultimately, the healing journey is not linear, and setbacks and challenges are inevitable. However, each obstacle presents an opportunity for growth and learning, and with perseverance and determination, the individual can emerge from their struggles stronger, wiser, and more resilient than ever before.

CHAPTER FIVE

Reflections

Looking Back,
Moving Forward

Reflections

As I revisited the pages of my memoir, I was struck by the raw authenticity and unwavering honesty with which I've shared my story. In bearing my heart on these pages, I invited you into the intimate places of my being, where the wounds of the past still linger, and the echoes of trauma reflect through the passages of time. From the tender innocence of my childhood to the tumultuous storms of adolescence and beyond, my narrative unfolds with a sorrow that resonates deeply within my heart. Each chapter is a testament to the resilience of my spirit, a testament to my courageous will to survive and thrive in the face of unimaginable adversity.

It's a journey marked by pain and resilience, darkness and light, moments of despair and triumph. It's a journey that has shaped me in ways I could have never imagined, molding me into the person I am today. Through the lens of my memory, you witnessed the complexities of my family dynamics, the wounds inflicted by those who were meant to protect me, and the enduring legacy of pain and betrayal. Yet, amidst the darkness, shines a beacon of hope - a flicker of light that illuminates the path toward healing and redemption. The unraveling of patterns, the search for love in all the wrong places, and my struggle to reclaim my position over my narrative are the threads that weave together the fabric of my life. With constant honesty and unwavering courage, I confront the troubles and fears of my past, forging a path toward self-discovery and self-empowerment.

One of the most profound realizations I've had on this journey is the power of vulnerability. For so long, I believed that strength meant endurance and that showing any sign of weakness was a sign of failure. But as I allowed myself to open up to share my story with others, I discovered that vulnerability is not a weakness but a source of immense strength. It takes courage to be vulnerable, to lay bare our deepest fears and insecurities, but in doing so, we allow others to see us for who we truly are. And in that exposure, we find connection, empathy, and healing.

Another lesson I've learned along the way is the importance of self-compassion. For so long, I carried the weight of shame and self-blame, believing I was somehow responsible for the pain I had endured. As I began to practice self-compassion, treating myself with the same kindness and understanding I would offer a friend—I realized that healing starts with forgiveness—both forgiving myself and others. It's a learning journey to embrace my imperfections, recognize my worthiness, and extend grace to myself in moments of struggle.

Perhaps the most transformative aspect of this journey has been learning to embrace the process - the messy, imperfect, nonlinear process of healing. It's a journey filled with highs and lows, with moments of clarity and confusion. Through the vessel of pain, I emerged transformed - a testament to the resilience of my spirit and the capacity for healing and growth.

There are days when the pain feels unbearable when the wounds of the past threaten to consume me. And yet, there are also moments of profound joy, and connection, moments when I catch a glimpse of the person I am becoming.

As I look back on the path I've traveled, I'm filled with gratitude - gratitude for the strength that has carried me through the darkest of times, gratitude for the love and support of those who have stood by my side, and appreciation for the resilience of my inner strength. And as I look ahead to the road that lies before me, I do so with hope - hope for continued healing, deeper connection, and a future filled with possibility. As my story is read, I hope it inspired all those who have known the depths of despair, guiding them toward the light of healing, transformation, and, ultimately, self-compassion. For in the end, it is not the scars that define us, but the courage to embrace our humanity, with all its flaws and imperfections, that sets us free.

In closing, I am reminded of Rumi's words: "The wound is the place where the light enters you." This quote addresses the idea that our vulnerabilities and wounds can lead to growth, healing, and transformation. May we all find the courage to embrace our wounds, to allow the light to illuminate the darkness, and to journey onward with open hearts and steadfastness. I am driven by a deep desire to break the generational cycles of trauma that have shaped my family's history. The late, great Maya Angelou is often quoted as saying, "As soon as healing takes place, go out and heal somebody else," though the authenticity of this quote has not been officially verified. These words have become my guiding light. I've come to realize that healing is a continuous journey that has the power to transform my life and inspire others along the way. Beginning this next chapter of my life, I am embarking on the journey toward earning my Doctor of Psychology (PsyD) degree, the theme *From Survivor to Healer* drives both my academic growth and personal development.

www.ingramcontent.com/pod-product-compliance
Lightning Source LLC
Chambersburg PA
CBHW060535130626
46553CB00002B/771